CONTENTS

How to use this guide	6
Distance checklist	11
Preface	12

INTRODUCTION
The Yorkshire Wolds Way story	15
Chalk landscape	16
History	17
Farming	20
Wildlife	23
Planning your walk	24
Waymarking	25
Weather	25
Equipment	29
Safety precautions	31

YORKSHIRE WOLDS WAY — 33

1 Hessle to South Cave	34
2 South Cave to Goodmanham	52
3 Goodmanham to Thixendale	72
4 Thixendale to Sherburn	98
5 Sherburn to Filey	114

USEFUL INFORMATION — 131
Transport	132
Accommodation	133
Tourist information centres	133
Local facilities	136
Useful addresses and telephone numbers	137
Nearby places of interest	140
Bibliography	141

Circular walks appear on pages 48, 69, 94, 112 and 126

How to use this guide

This guide to the 79-mile (127-kilometre) Yorkshire Wolds Way
is in three parts:
- The introduction, with an historical background to the area
and advice for walkers.
- The Way itself, split into five chapters, with maps opposite
the description for each route section. The distances noted with
each chapter represent the total length of the Yorkshire Wolds
Way, including sections through towns and villages. This part
of the guide also includes information on places of interest as
well as a number of short walks that can be taken around parts
of the path. Key sites are numbered both in the text and on the
maps to make it easier to follow the route description.
- The last part includes useful information such as local
transport, accommodation and organisations involved with the
Yorkshire Wolds Way.

The maps have been prepared by the Ordnance Survey for this
Trail Guide using 1:25 000 Explorer™ maps as a base. The line of
the Yorkshire Wolds Way is shown in yellow, with the status of
each section of the trail – footpath or bridleway, for example –
shown in green underneath (see key on inside front cover). These
rights of way markings also indicate the precise alignment of the
Yorkshire Wolds Way, which you should follow. In some cases, the
yellow line on these maps may show a route that is different from
that shown on older maps; you are recommended to follow the
yellow route in this guide, which will be the route that is
waymarked with the distinctive acorn symbol 🌰 used for all
National Trails. Any parts of the Yorkshire Wolds Way that may be
difficult to follow on the ground are clearly highlighted in the
route description, and important points to watch for are marked
with letters in each chapter, both in the text and on the maps.
*Some maps start on a right-hand page and continue on the left-hand page
– black arrows (➡) at the edge of the maps indicate the start point.*

Should there be a need to divert the Yorkshire Wolds Way
from the route shown in this guide, for maintenance work or
because the route has had to be changed, you are advised to
follow any waymarks or signs along the path.

titles so far published in this series

Offa's Dyke Path South
Offa's Dyke Path North
Cleveland Way
The Ridgeway
Pennine Way South
Pennine Way North
Pembrokeshire Coast Path
South Downs Way
North Downs Way
Yorkshire Wolds Way
The Thames Path
Hadrian's Wall Path

Peddars Way and Norfolk
   Coast Path
Pennine Bridleway:
   Derbyshire to the
   South Pennines
Glyndŵr's Way

South West Coast Path
Minehead to Padstow
Padstow to Falmouth
Falmouth to Exmouth
Exmouth to Poole

YORKSHIRE WOLDS WAY

Roger Ratcliffe

AURUM PRESS

The
Countryside
Agency

Acknowledgements

I wish to recognise the Ramblers' Association, East Yorkshire and Derwent Area, which first conceived the idea of a Yorkshire Wolds Way, and the footpath officers of Humberside County Council and North Yorkshire County Council, whose hard work made it a reality. These groups also helped me with my research.

Roger Ratcliffe was formerly Environment Correspondent of the *Yorkshire Post* and North of England Correspondent of the *Sunday Times*. He currently runs his own publishing business.

The publishers acknowledge with thanks the help provided by the Yorkshire Wolds Way Special Project Office, Alan Staniforth, in preparing this revised edition.

First published as *Wolds Way* in 1992
by Aurum Press Ltd, 25 Bedford Avenue, London WC1B 3AT
This revised edition published in 2004
by Aurum Press Ltd in association with the Countryside Agency

Text copyright © 1992, 2004 by Aurum Press Ltd and the Countryside Agency
Photographs © 1992, 2004 by the Countryside Agency
The photographs on the cover, pages 2-3, 54-5, 82-3, 96-7, 102-3, 110-1, 134-5
are by Mike Kipling. The photographs on pages 14 and 65 are by Tessa Bunney.
All other photographs are by Ian Carstairs.

A catalogue record for this book is available from the British Library.

ISBN 1 85410 986 3

1 3 5 7 9 10 8 6 4 2
2004 2006 2008 2007 2005

Book design by Robert Updegraff
Printed and bound in Italy by Printer Trento Srl

Cover photograph: *A characteristic Yorkshire Wolds landscape at the heart of the National Trail.*
Title-page photograph: *Dry, steep-sided valleys are a typical feature of the Yorkshire Wolds Way.*

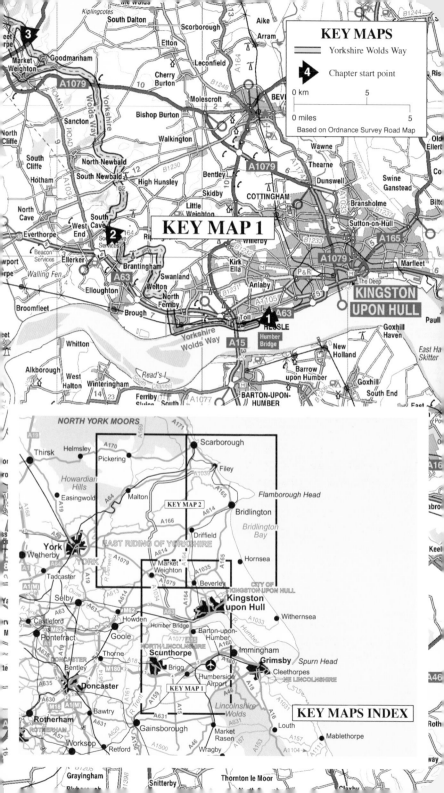

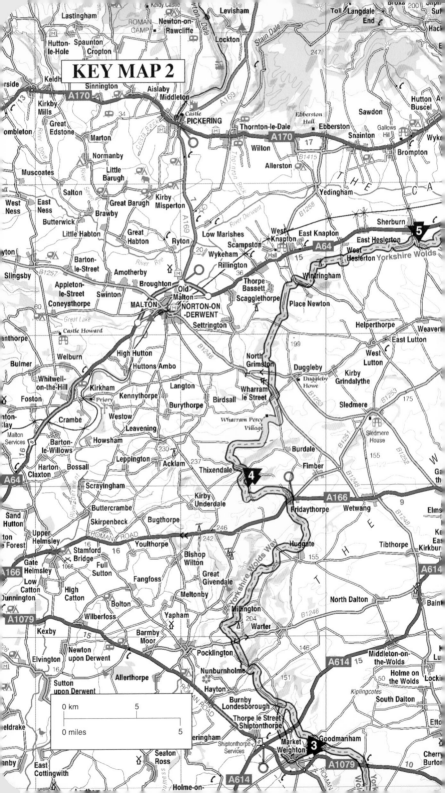

Skidby Mill, near Beverley, the last surviving windmill to be found in the north-east.

Distance Checklist

This list will assist you in calculating the distances between your proposed overnight accommodation and in checking your progress along the walk.

location	approx. distance from previous location	
	miles	km
Hessle	0	0
North Ferriby	3.1	5.0
Welton	3.5	5.6
Brantingham	4.2	6.7
South Cave	2.1	3.4
Newbald	5.2	8.4
Goodmanham	5.8	9.3
(Market Weighton – from Newbald)	(6.7)	(10.8)
Londesborough	2.4	3.9
(Londesborough – from Market Weighton)	(2.7)	(4.3)
Nunburnholme	2.5	4.0
Millington	2.7	4.3
Huggate	5.9	9.5
Fridaythorpe	2.5	4.0
Thixendale	4.1	6.6
Wharram le Street	5.3	8.5
Settrington Beacon	3.7	6.0
Wintringham	2.7	4.3
Sherburn	6.8	10.9
Ganton	3.0	4.8
Staxton Wold	3.2	5.1
Muston	6.5	10.5
Filey	1.5	2.4

Preface

The Yorkshire Wolds Way gives access to a landscape that has remained unchanged for many years – a landscape of real contrasts, from wide open field tops with views which stretch for miles to hidden, secretive dry valleys that have their own distinctive and unique charm.

Your journey along this National Trail will take you to attractive villages, with traditional country pubs, and allow you to drink in the 'big skies' which are all around you. You can experience them on long trips, as part of a circular walk or simply on an afternoon out.

Promoted and funded primarily by the Countryside Agency, the Yorkshire Wolds Way is maintained and waymarked by local authorities and is managed by a Trail Manager who looks after its entire length. National Trails are all recognisable by the use of the distinctive acorn symbol, a quality mark which signals that you are on the right route.

I hope you will use this guide to help you find the peace and quiet that is so high on the agenda in this area and that it will add to your enjoyment of the countryside and your understanding of this special area.

Ewen Cameron
Chairman
Countryside Agency

PART ONE

INTRODUCTION

It is ironic that lovers of unspoilt countryside in northern England often eschew national parks like the Yorkshire Dales and North York Moors. Instead, they find peace and quiet and spiritual renewal in the Yorkshire Wolds, where no Act of Parliament has been necessary to safeguard the landscape's essential character. These gently rolling chalk hills with their wooded slopes and deep green, almost secretive, valleys have avoided the coffee-table book treatment. Few coach parties hog their narrow lanes, crocodiles of walkers are rarely met on the springy footpaths, and the pretty, pantile-roofed houses in Wolds villages are not second homes or holiday cottages.

There is no better way to discover the many historic and picturesque gems in these hills than by following the Yorkshire Wolds Way along its 79 miles (127 km). From Hessle Haven, beside the gritty brown Humber, to the airy cliffs above Filey, the National Trail links virtually all of the interesting features to be found in this last great thrust of English chalk. There is the mighty Humber Bridge; there are wonderful abandoned railway lines to walk along, or the route of England's oldest horse race; the best-preserved deserted medieval village is at Wharram Percy; and a most fascinating geological feature on the English coast is Filey Brigg, climax of the Yorkshire Wolds Way.

In between, there are beautiful woodland walks, bracing field tops with breathtaking views and the dry chalk valleys that have remained largely unchanged for centuries.

It is a landscape that has been described as 'a piece of southern England in the North', for it is difficult to imagine a greater contrast with the exposed heather moors, wild peaty bogs and gritstone fells that one associates with northern England. Being mostly Grade 1 agricultural land, there is no reason to fear that these splendid chalk wolds will ever be encroached upon by developments like new towns and industrial estates.

The Yorkshire Wolds Way demands the use of tarmac lanes at several places but these lanes, most of them rarely used by traffic, are an essential feature of the hills, and walkers should relish them as such. Most have very wide grass verges, since they were old drove roads, making walking both safe and comfortable.

All the walks described in this book will appeal to every level of walking ability. There are short sections, and longer ones for those who like to cover a lot of ground. One thing is certain – even the most accomplished of National Trail walkers, perhaps with fresh memories of the wilder sections of Offa's Dyke or the ancient Ridgeway, will not fail to be seduced by the placid Yorkshire Wolds countryside.

The Yorkshire Wolds Way story

The formation of long-distance footpaths in England and Wales was very much a product of the 1960s expansion of leisure time, disposable income and interest in the countryside. Following the Pennine Way's opening in 1965, there was pressure from ramblers for a number of other routes that would traverse a range of hills while linking a series of historic and scenic treasures.

Woodland aconites are amongst the first flowers to appear in early spring.

The Wolds Way, as it was called until the word 'Yorkshire' was added to the title in 2003, was one such continuous footpath. The idea came from the Ramblers' Association, East Yorkshire and Derwent Area, whose members had long appreciated the beauties of the Yorkshire Wolds. Their proposal was put to the National Parks Commission (forerunner of the Countryside Commission – now the Countryside Agency) in 1967 and within a year it had been approved in principle by the new Commission and by the East Riding County Council. The route would begin on the Humber shore at North Ferriby and finish at the East Riding county boundary just north of Filey Brigg.

The first section to open was a 4-mile (6.5-km) path through Goodmanham and Londesborough, which was officially inaugurated by Lord Halifax, then Lord Lieutenant of the East Riding, in November 1973. But it was not until 26th July 1977 that the Countryside Commission formally proposed a complete route. It had taken 10 years to get just one small stretch of the National Trail officially opened and waymarked; it was to take another five years to get agreement over the rest of the Yorkshire Wolds Way.

The route that was finally agreed included an extension to Hessle Haven, at its southernmost end, and a link with Market Weighton. The most difficult sections to secure were at the northern end, between Thixendale and Filey, and about 10 miles of new rights-of-way had to be created. At last, the official route was opened on 2nd October 1982, at a ceremony performed by a major Wolds landowner, Lord Middleton, at Fridaythorpe.

Chalk landscape

Chalk underlies virtually all of the Yorkshire Wolds Way. Only the final stretch of walking on the boulder clay cliffs at Filey, and the anomalous black reef of lower calcareous gritstone that forms Filey Brigg, provide a contrast in scenery.

The Yorkshire Wolds are, in fact, the northernmost extremity of a continuous band of chalk extending from South Devon. It rolls through Dorset, eastward to form such national landmarks as the Seven Sisters and the White Cliffs of Dover, then ripples through Sussex and Kent as the North and South Downs, dipping under the Thames and London. It also thrusts through Wiltshire and Berkshire and the Chilterns of Buckinghamshire, reaching through Norfolk but again disappearing from view at The Wash to reappear as the Lincolnshire Wolds.

Cut by the mighty Humber, the chalk finally emerges to create the Yorkshire Wolds before terminating as the scenic *pièce de résistance* of Flamborough Head and the high-rise seabird colonies of Bempton Cliffs.

Chalk was formed between 65 and 140 million years ago and is composed of the bones and shells of countless minute creatures that accumulated when earth movements reduced the sea level over the infant British landscape. The white mud compressed and hardened, and was squeezed and eroded by volcanic action and the creation of new rivers. The final polish of softly rounded hills and dry valleys was provided by the last Ice Age. And the rest of what we know today as classic English chalk downland scenery was formed by people – the sweet chalk pastures, the steep meadow banks, the well-cultivated and grazed terrain of some of the most fertile land in Europe.

Water is quickly absorbed by chalk, which means that conditions underfoot are never wet for long because the land quickly dries out after rain. This absorption also deprives the landscape of many springs and water courses. A curious characteristic of chalk downland is the streams that usually run underground but occasionally break to the surface. In the Yorkshire Wolds they are known as 'races', the best-known being the Gypsey Race, which runs from Duggleby, just off the Yorkshire Wolds Way, to Bridlington. In southern and western England they are known as 'bournes'. However, in this part of the country water abstraction has meant that the 'races' are a much rarer sight now than they once were.

History

Some of the oldest cultivated landscape is to be found in chalk downs. Mesolithic tribes from the Continent arrived in southern England as the ice sheets melted and spread north. They lived off the fish and wild animals to be found in the Vale of Pickering to the north of the Wolds.

Around the year 3250 BC came yet more invaders from the Mediterranean who brought with them the earliest farming skills. They had no need for the hunting grounds of marshes but colonised the fertile hills, developing a patchwork of small fields. Thus the Wolds, which have so few habitations today, were very much alive 4,000 years ago. Later settlers arrived from France, tribes of warriors with chieftains whose remains were buried with chariots in great barrows – their main legacy to today's landscape.

Looking north-east, across the Wolds vrom above Nunburnholme.

The Romans arrived in about AD 71. Their principal camp was west of the Wolds at *Eboracum*, the embryonic city of York. They also built a signal station above Filey Brigg, at the end of the Yorkshire Wolds Way, to raise the alarm should the Angles invade from the sea. Indeed, the Angles did just that in the 5th century, but by then the Romans had finished with Britain.

The Saxons, and later the Danes, laid the foundation for much of what you see in the Wolds today – names like Brantingham and Goodmanham are Saxon, while the numerous villages and farm names ending in 'by' and 'thorpe' are a reminder of the Danes. It is thought that many field boundaries, still in use, were first laid out by these pre-Conquest settlers.

Early medieval times were a turbulent period in the area's history. Many people were driven off the land by the Norman barons. The Black Death also caused thousands of casualties and virtually wiped out some settlements, the most famous being Wharram Percy. Later, land enclosures meant that the Wolds were turned over to sheep rearing. Cereal growing, which is the dominant agricultural activity today, began in the 18th century, and since that time hedges may have been grubbed out to enlarge a field but, essentially, you see the same type of landscape that existed 200 years ago.

Farming

The Yorkshire Wolds is one of the most intensively farmed areas of Britain. About 95 per cent of the land is arable, the main production being cereal crops, such as winter and spring/winter barley. About one-third of the Wolds comprises grazing pastures or oilseed rape production, with a smaller acreage devoted to pea vining. In the 1980s the Wolds became one of Britain's largest producers of oilseed rape.

The soil quality, although good throughout the Wolds, is richest on the southernmost slopes fronting the Humber. The loam is medium to heavy, and the presence of large numbers of chalk stones and pebbles keeps it well drained.

Although the days of the vast sheep walks have long gone, the principal livestock is still sheep. Up to 200,000 lambs and ewes are herded, with most of the common breeds being represented. The Wolds are also used for dairy and beef cattle production, and the predominant breeds are black and white Friesian and Holstein with a few herds of Charolais and Limousin.

The fine Norman doorway of St Nicholas Church, situated in the village of North Newbald.

Forestry work under way in Deep Dale Plantation, which lies above the village of Wintringham.

There are some extremely large farms in the Yorkshire Wolds. These were created during the land enclosures of 1750–1850. Smaller farmsteads exist only beside the villages.

Because the Yorkshire Wolds Way runs almost entirely across agricultural land, it is necessary to be meticulous in your observance of the Country Code (see the inside of the back cover). In particular, you should keep to footpaths, be extremely careful with matches or cigarette ends, keep dogs on leads, close all gates behind you, not tamper with machinery, and not pick or destroy crops. Several stretches of the Yorkshire Wolds Way were created with the consent and co-operation of farmers and you should repay them by behaving responsibly.

Wildlife

Geology is usually the key to an area's wildlife, and chalk downland has some of the most distinctive flora and fauna in the British landscape. Well-drained banks and fields with calcium-rich soils in areas like the Yorkshire Wolds provide ideal conditions for flowers that require lime for their survival, such as harebells, bee orchids, cowslips, buttercups, shepherd's purse, wild thyme and wild basil.

These, in turn, attract colourful butterflies in summer, like the orange tip, red admiral and the common blue. The uncultivated grasses provide nesting places for skylarks, the seeds of tall grasses are food for goldfinches. There are bank voles, which, of course, attract the kestrel, and stoats and weasels lurk in the hedge bottoms. The open fields have hares, partridges, lapwings, yet more musical skylarks, meadow-pipits, and noisy flocks of rooks, gulls and jackdaws appear when the earth is being ploughed.

The hawthorn hedgerows that accompany the Yorkshire Wolds Way for so many miles have their own special inhabitants. All of the common small birds are present throughout the year, as well as family groups of long-tailed tits and the occasional raiding sparrowhawk. Blood-red poppies thrive in the difficult corners out of reach of the plough and, if you rest awhile at a field gate, it is possible you might see a little owl.

The beech woodland sections are often fragrant with honeysuckle, while forget-me-nots, red campion, bluebells and primroses carpet the floor in season. Where the footpath joins a metalled lane, the banks are piled with cow parsley in summer. The woodland and some hedge banks also contain a number of fungi in late summer and autumn, but be warned that most of them are poisonous and the best advice is that, unless you know the subject, leave them alone!

The start and finish of the Yorkshire Wolds Way provide their own distinctive wildlife showcases. On the Humber foreshore there are many wading birds and feeding ducks, while the Yorkshire coast supports most species of British seabirds and, if your skills at bird identification are up to it, many irregular visitors on migration.

Planning your walk

Virtually the only decision you need to make before you set off from home, if it is your intention to complete the Yorkshire Wolds Way, is in which direction you should walk. There is no reason why, if it appeals to you, you should not begin on the cliffs at Filey and walk south to just east of the Humber Bridge, but there are some good reasons for beginning at the Humber and ending on the coast. One is that it is usually better to walk with the sun on your back, especially on bright days when walking towards it can be dazzling and something of a strain on the eyes. Another south–north justification is to do with the landscape itself. From its inauspicious beginnings on the muddy Humber bank, the beauty of the scenery intensifies by the day. Filey Brigg is a fine place to finish your 'Walk on the Wolds' but if you can spare an extra day to walk along the magnificent chalk cliffs of Bempton and Flamborough and on to Bridlington you will complete an arc of chalk scenery that is second to none in England. This book describes the route from south to north.

The Yorkshire Wolds Way is not one of the 'heavyweights' of long-distance walking in Britain and even a novice should accomplish it with ease. At no point is the terrain difficult; indeed, with the exception of about half a dozen short inclines where the path climbs out of chalk dales on to the airy Wolds, the whole of the route is on level valley bottoms or open fields.

The route is described in five chapters, each one terminating where accommodation can be found. The first (Hessle to South Cave) covers approximately 13 miles (21 km) in length, which should be just enough if you have driven or travelled by train from home that same day. Public transport provision at the start of the footpath and on the final section makes it possible to do these walks and return to your starting point on the same day. But the stages in between are across areas where rural transport provision is poor and these sections are best done (unless you are with a friend and arrange a transport pick-up at the end) as part of the continuous route.

If you estimate walking at a pace that covers 3 miles (5 km) an hour, your morning start on the sections between Market Weighton and Filey should be no later than 9 a.m. if you wish to arrive at your lodgings in time for an evening meal.

Having decided on your programme, it is wise to book your accommodation in advance (see page 133 for details).

Overall, the Yorkshire Wolds Way is perfect for a week's holiday. If you start from home on Monday morning, for example, you can easily cover the distance as described in this book by Friday teatime and, after a night's rest, return on the Saturday.

It is best to do the walk in spring, summer or autumn – all have their own special magic. Winter, apart from being scenically rather dull, has the added disadvantage of fewer accommodation options, as many bed and breakfast guesthouses operate only from Easter to October, and public transport can be even harder to find.

Waymarking

Because of the great need to keep to paths on agricultural land, the footpath is well signposted, especially at junctions with other rights of way and at roads. The signposts are clearly marked 'Yorkshire Wolds Way' or, more often, just 'Wolds Way' and bear the Countryside Agency's National Trail symbol, a stylised acorn. The acorn is used in other places where confirmation of the correct path is required.

Weather

It is well known that eastern England enjoys lower rainfall than the west side, but that is little consolation to the walker whose long-planned holiday on the Yorkshire Wolds Way coincides with a period of unremitting downpours. However, the weather records of the region do offer a limited guide to anyone making some advance arrangements for a week on the footpath. April, May and June are generally drier than July and August, then in September and October there are often many days of unbroken fine weather. Between November and Easter the Wolds can suffer some of the deepest snowdrifts in England, when the wind turns to the east and cuts like a scythe.

The winter snowfields that often cut off Huggate from the outside world.

The contrast between Wolds weather and that found on the coast can sometimes be quite remarkable. On scorching days inland, the seaside can be often cooled by sea breezes, which also produce cloudy skies. Also on the coast, sea-frets (wet mists coming inland from the sea) gather on windless days when the air is warmer than the sea. These can move onshore and in these circumstances extra care is required if walking on the cliffs at Filey.

Before setting out on the Yorkshire Wolds Way, it might be useful to check the area's weather either on the web at www.metoffice.com or by telephoning Weathercall UK on 09068 232 770 or AA Weatherwatch on 09003 444 900. Both are premium rate services.

Ripening barley along the western escarpment of the Yorkshire Wolds Way.

Equipment

In guides to other National Trails this section might begin with advice such as 'a good pair of walking boots is essential' but, in the case of the Yorkshire Wolds Way, there are no sections of footpath where they are absolutely essential. The route lies entirely across agricultural land, much of it on gently undulating fields, and the only point at which you could conceivably require a firm grip is if you descend to Filey Brigg and the sometimes slimy surface of the Brigg itself. A pair of lightweight walking boots is adequate. They offer some degree of protection on slippery surfaces and will not feel like lead weights after the first day's walk.

A possible alternative could be a pair of training shoes that you do not mind getting a bid mud-splattered, and a pair of lightweight wellies. The latter are especially useful after rain, when some sections of the footpath are muddy – the wellies are easily washed at the next large puddle! Take several pairs of socks and, since long-distance walking puts considerable strain on your feet, wear a soft, inner pair and a harder outer pair to allow the feet's perspiration to be well absorbed.

Whenever you choose to walk, waterproofs are essential, and their effectiveness depends on what you can afford to buy. Breathable fabrics like Gore-tex, while costly, stop you feeling as if you are walking inside a plastic bin-liner. The once-obligatory extra sweater is now often replaced by a garment in one of the fleecy, ultra-insulating materials on the market. Outside the summer season it is best to take gloves and warm headwear. The best overall advice is to be prepared for the rain and the cold.

Since there are limited refreshment stops *en route*, you should take a flask or water bottle and fill it with your requirements before setting out each day. Most farms encountered along the route have outdoor water taps, but ask first before using them.

Do not forget the items that you hope never to need. It is not a waste of time lugging a few emergency tools in your rucksack. Place them in a convenient pocket or position for quick access. Essentials are a compass, in case you stray off the path in mist or darkness; a torch and whistle; a small first-aid kit; some high-energy food such as glucose, mint cake, dried fruit or chocolate; a survival bag, especially if walking alone, in case you accidentally fall on a remote stretch of the path; and some hay-fever medication in spring and summer, if you are a sufferer.

The old lifeboat station at Coble Landing, Filey. The lifeboat is towed to and from the sea by tractor.

Safety precautions

The Yorkshire Wolds Way has been divided into five different sections in this book and each one should be within the abilities of the average walker carrying a rucksack of around 30 lb (14 kg). Between the overnight stops, villages and houses are rare, so make sure that you are equipped for any emergency.

There are only a few parts of the footpath where slips or falls might occur. These are on some of the steep banks climbing out of the chalk dales, such as Rabbit Warren and Nettle Dale, near Millington; the ascent of Deep Dale from Wintringham; or at Filey Brigg and the nearby cliffs. However, only carelessness could result in an accident.

A short section of the path along the Humber foreshore at North Ferriby is liable to flooding at the time of high spring tides, but a safe alternative is described in this book. If you wish to explore Filey Brigg, check the state of the tide (ask at the tourist information centre in John Street, Filey) and avoid it altogether when the tide is high. You should also bypass it if a sea-fret blankets the coast. Along the cliff footpath, do not stray too near the edge. If you want to get a wide view of the coast use the good, safe vantage points.

If you do have an emergency, look in this guide book for the location of the nearest farm, telephone box or village. If you are able to send someone to raise the alarm, give this book to that person, once they have established your exact location.

PART TWO

Yorkshire Wolds Way

1 Hessle to South Cave

via North Ferriby and Welton
13 miles (20.9 km)

For those walkers travelling from home to reach the beginning of the Yorkshire Wolds Way and thus getting a late start on the footpath, this opening section should be easily completed in time to reach overnight accommodation and an evening meal at a reasonable hour. Until Welton is reached it is level walking although, on a fine day, you will not wish to hurry the 3-mile (5-km) stretch that partners the fascinating Humber Estuary **1** (see page 42).

Given the overall dominance of the Humber Bridge **3** it may appear a little odd that the official start of the National Trail is at Hessle Haven, about half a mile (0.8km) to the east. The reasons for this are linked to the establishment of the route in the early 1970s. Whether you arrive in Hessle by train or bus it is only a short walk to join the Yorkshire Wolds Way opposite the old Ferryboat Inn **A** or at the new sculpted waymarker **B** closer

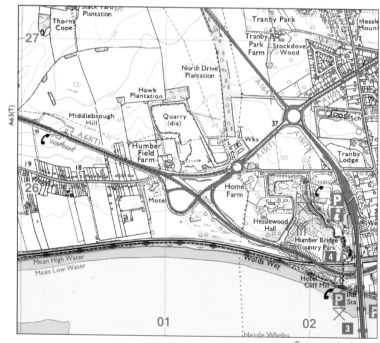

Contours are given in metres
The vertical interval is 5m

to the Humber Bridge, the brother of which you will eventually meet on Filey Brigg.

On the opposite bank of Hessle Haven was the site **2** of one of the last yards on the Humber where locally distinctive keel boats were built in the early part of the last century. Turn right and follow Jeans Walk along the bank of the Humber. Just before the bridge you will pass the stone sculpture **B** which marks a more photogenic start to your walk to the North Sea. The white pebbles and boulders along the river bank are a sure sign that the chalk Wolds are not far away.

A handgate gives access to the shore to pass in front of The Country Park Inn. The route then joins a wide track bordered by the Hull–Selby railway line (opened 1840) on the right.

The area around the bridge contains a Tourist Information Centre, many car parking spaces and visitor facilities, including information boards explaining the Humber's history and wildlife. Once under the giant legs (510 feet/156 metres high with foundations 26 feet/8 metres deep) you will see the frontage of the Humber Bridge Country Park **4**, which includes

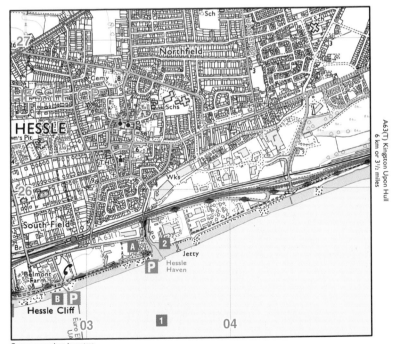

Contours are given in metres
The vertical interval is 5m

Hessle Haven, near the start of the Yorkshire Wolds Way, is an ever-changing hive of indust

vity.

the ruin of an old five-sail windmill. The park was established around a chalk quarry and opened in 1986.

A significant number of barges still ply the estuary, carrying bulk loads like timber, quarry materials and fertilisers to and from the smaller wharfs on the Ouse and Trent. Bigger vessels include tankers and car transporters, the latter bound for Goole – a major port of entry for imported vehicles. If you are lucky, you might see a Humber keel, a flat-bottomed craft with a square rig that was for centuries the traditional means of transporting cargoes of coal, grain and other bulk goods on the river. There is still one preserved Humber keel, the *Comrade*. Also, look out for *Amy Howson*, the sole surviving example of a Humber sloop, flat-bottomed but with fore-and-aft rig. Both are operated by the Humber Keel & Sloop Preservation Society.

When you reach the reed pond **C** care should be taken when there is a high tide or the river is in spate as the path along the shore may be dangerous. In this event turn right on the alternative route, turn left on reaching the tarmac road then right **D** up Humber Road. Cross the railway bridge and continue ahead up Station Road and Narrow Lane to turn left **E** along High Street, which becomes Melton Road, and follow this to rejoin the Way at the A63(T) **F**.

If the shore is clear, however, continue ahead to where the trees met the river **G**. It was near here **5,** in 1937, that two brothers spotted some wood protruding from the mud. When they dug deeper they found the remains of three Bronze Age boats, constructed from bevelled oak planks and moss caulking bound with yew withies. One of the brothers made further finds along the river bank during the 1940s and the 1960s. Recent research funded by English Heritage dates one of these vessels back nearly 4,000 years, making it one of the oldest of its kind yet discovered in western Europe. Now regarded as one of the most significant archaeological finds in Britain, these 50-foot (16-metre)-long vessels would have been paddled by up to 18 oarsmen, possibly assisted by a sail. Originally thought to have been used as Humber ferry boats, it is now apparent that these boats would also have been used for sea-going trade.

Go up the timber steps and follow the path into Long Plantation. You emerge on to the main road **F**. It is a dangerous road to cross, so walkers should use the footbridge 550 yards (500 metres) to the left and return to the path leading into Terrace Plantation. Here begins your first gentle climb on a Wolds hillside.

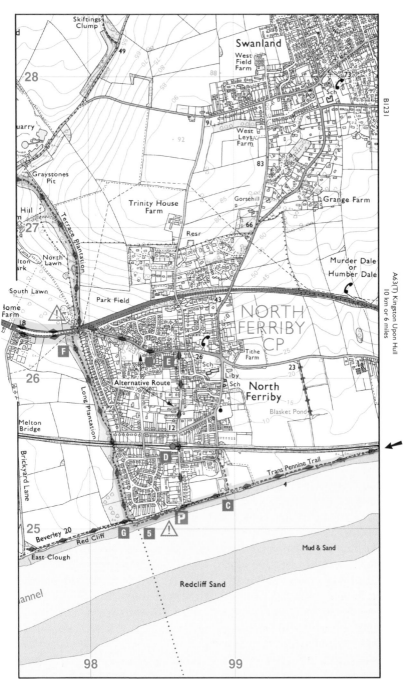

Contours are given in metres
The vertical interval is 5m

39

1 km or ½ mile
A63(T) Elloughton

Contours are given in metres
The vertical interval is 5m

Cross the metalled road **H** and follow the track past the huge chasm of Melton Bottom Quarry **6**. Look out for a left turn into Bow Plantation. Turn down the road **I** which descends to the village of Welton **7**, your earliest experience of a Wolds village. It also happens to be one of the prettiest, especially around St Helen's Church and the mill stream.

The Yorkshire Wolds Way continues up Dale Road **J** to one of the many secluded stretches of the footpath. Pass the modern houses, Welton Lodge and Welton Mill, continue beyond Dale Cottage to Welton Dale. This is lined with trees and is a gorgeous sun trap in summer. A gate gives access to Welton Wold Plantation through which, up to the left, you may catch a glimpse of the domed mausoleum (no public access) built in 1818 by the erstwhile occupants of Welton House, the Raikes family.

Cross the concrete road **K** and turn right inside the field edge and after a short distance turn left. At the end of the conifer plantation you will have a good view of the impressive Wauldby Manor Farm **8** and as you approach Wauldby Dam you may also spot the little church amongst the trees. Turn left then sharp right by the farm cottages and walk on a gently undulating track until you reach a junction, where you turn left **L**. The high hawthorn hedges hereabouts are some of the most impressive in the area. At the road junction go straight ahead and where the road turns sharp left **M** continue ahead along the broad track past Long Plantation. The track merges into a tarmac lane from which there are impressive views over flat terrain towards the industrial towns of South and West Yorkshire. As you descend the steep lane look out for a path on the right **N** which drops down towards Brantingham Church. If you wish to visit beautiful Brantingham **9** itself, continue down the road and turn left into the village. Most impressive is Brantingham Hall, a 2½-storey

40

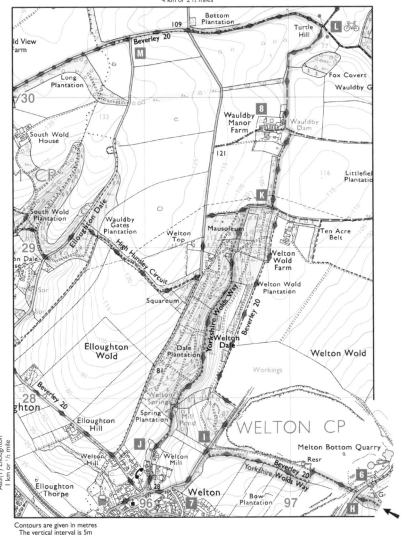

Contours are given in metres
The vertical interval is 5m

red brick house overlooking the village pond. Further south is a Gothic war memorial, built from an assortment of features from Hull's Victorian Town Hall (replaced in 1914 by the Guildhall) and described by one expert as 'lovably awful'.

All Saints Brantingham **10**, nestling snugly in its wooded dale, has the most picturesque setting of any church encountered along the Yorkshire Wolds Way, with the possible exception of the ruined St Martin's at Wharram Percy. Bits of it can

41

be dated to the 13th century, but most of what you see today can be attributed to a restoration by G. E. Street, paid for by the wealthy Sykes family of Sledmere.

Continue up the road past the church and at the first sweeping bend **O** turn left to follow the path into the forest. At the top of the hill drop down towards Woodale Farm **11**, turning right just before the buildings. In a short distance branch off to the left through a small handgate and climb uphill to reach Mount Airy Farm **12**. Immediately past the farm buildings turn sharp left and follow the tarmac road downhill to join the road **P** into South Cave. It is at this point that those seeking accommodation or refreshment in South Cave should leave the Yorkshire Wolds Way.

The Humber

Often referred to, erroneously, as the 'River' Humber, this mighty estuary **1** is formed by the confluence of the Rivers Trent and Yorkshire Ouse, which between them drain 9,650 square miles (25,000 square km), equivalent to one-fifth of England's land surface.

The estuary was created more than 70 million years ago when the chalk beds, composed of millions of tiny marine organisms, were thrust to the surface by movement of the earth's crust, and the water – which had once covered them – drained through several massive channels to form new seas. One of the biggest of such channels was the Humber, leaving what became the Lincolnshire Wolds on the south bank and the Yorkshire Wolds on the north. Originally, it drained into the North Sea on the eastern fringe of Hull, but the last Ice Age dumped huge amounts of boulder clay to form what today is known as Holderness, a vast flat area running from Hull to the chalk headland at Flamborough.

It was through the mouth of the Humber that the first settlers arrived from the Continent. Simple Bronze Age boats hollowed out from oak trees by fire and crude tools have been found (as evinced by the Brigg boat, found on the Ancholme, which flows into the Humber on the south bank), as well as the more sophisticated vessels made from huge oak planks sewn together with yew withies (as shown by the discovery of the North Ferriby boats **5**.)

It was by the Humber that the invaders who were to make the earliest impact on the Wolds, the Parisii, arrived from France around 300 BC. They cultivated the landscape and left traces that can still be seen as earthworks near Huggate and Millington, and

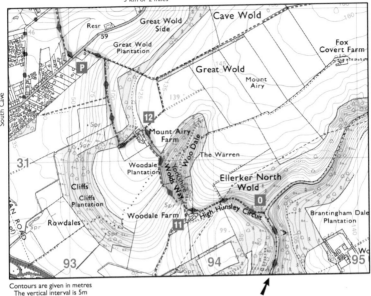

Contours are given in metres
The vertical interval is 5m

a number of chariot burials of their chieftains. Romans and Vikings all used the Humber during their respective invasions; it was the northern frontier of the Roman Empire at one time. Also it was from Immingham Creek, on the south bank, that the earliest Pilgrim Fathers sailed in 1608.

Since the Industrial Revolution, the Humber has been one of the most important shipping lanes in Europe, with navigation schemes connecting the port of Hull with the great inland cities of Sheffield, Nottingham and Leeds and, via the Leeds–Liverpool canal, with the west coast.

Cargo vessels still navigate the gritty brown waters, but the channels and sandbanks are dynamic and have been changing for thousands of years. The shipping lanes have to be regularly altered and river mariners treat the Humber with great respect.

The Humber Bridge and its setting

The Humber Bridge **3** is arguably the most spectacular man-made structure encountered on any National Trail in Britain (historians may prefer the structure which gives its name to the Hadrian's Wall Path National Trail). End to end, from the cliffs above the Hessle foreshore to the outskirts of Barton-on-Humber on the south bank, it reaches 7,283 1/2 feet or just under 1 1/2 miles (2.2 km) long. Its most important dimension is the single span

Dusk arrives over the Humber Bridge, one of the world's longest single-span bridges.

between the two giant piers: 4,626 feet (1,411 metres), which makes it one of the world's longest single-span suspension bridges. Toll-paying traffic on dual two-lane carriageways and two pedestrian/cycle paths pass some 150 feet (46 metres) above the estuary. Exceptionally keen walkers can arrive at the start of the Yorkshire Wolds Way via the Viking Way long-distance foot-path, which begins at Oakham in Leicestershire and ends 140 miles (225 km) north on the other side of the Humber Bridge.

A regular ferry crossing of the Humber was established in 1825 and operated between Hull Corporation Pier and New Holland until just before the bridge was opened by the Queen on 17th July 1981. Plans for a railway tunnel in the 1870s and a road bridge in the 1930s collapsed through lack of funds, and the present structure, which cost more than £90 million to build and has since run up debts many times that amount in interest charges, is commonly claimed to have been an enticement to electors during a Hull by-election in the 1960s. Its construction was considered essential to the creation of the new county of Humberside (population 850,000) in 1974, formed from the old East Riding and part of North Lincolnshire.

To the immediate west of the north bank pier is the Humber Bridge Country Park **4**, a 48-acre (19-hectare) site containing meadows, woodlands, ponds, cliffs, an old mill, nature trails, information centre, café, toilets, etc. The park was formed from an old chalk quarry, first worked in 1317. Access is immediately off the Yorkshire Wolds Way by clearly signposted foot-paths leading away from the shore.

Barton Clay Pits

Extending either side of the Humber Bridge on the south bank are the Barton Clay Pits, a 5-mile (8-km) strip of now largely flooded clay workings. Clay from this area has been used extensively in the past for making bricks and roofing tiles. The industry steadily declined after the First World War and today only two tile works remain. The flooded pits have now become havens for wildlife and recreational activities. At the western end is Far Ings, an attractive nature reserve managed by the Lincolnshire Wildlife Trust, while to the east is an 86-acre country park and local nature reserve, Waters' Edge, operated by North Lincolnshire Council. This site is a wonderful habitat for birds, many of which nest here. The nationally rare bittern can be seen over the Park on most days between April and September. Walkways, bird hides and visitor facilities make this a very attractive area to visit, all in the shadow of the mighty Humber Bridge. Also in the area are several fisheries and sites for sailing and windsurfing. Close by is a former rope works which now houses changing exhibitions of contemporary art and craft.

Humber birdlife

It is on the first stretch of the Yorkshire Wolds Way that the greatest variety of birdlife may be seen. The Humber **1** is recognised as one of the most important bird feeding grounds on the east coast. Wading birds that are present at most times of the year include dunlin, redshank and oystercatcher, joined at the spring and autumn migration periods by large numbers of knot, sanderling, curlew, grey and ringed plover, bar-tailed godwit and perhaps the odd rarity, all of them probing the intertidal mud for bivalve molluscs and polychaete worms. Species of duck include mallard and shelduck, plus the occasional teal and wigeon. In addition, up the estuary some 10,000 pink-footed geese winter annually and some wander downstream. The shore between the bridge and North Ferriby is hunted by short-eared owls and kestrels and there is often a solitary heron for company. The Humber Bridge Country Park **4** beside the bridge is good for the common species of warblers in spring and summer.

Welton

The village of Welton **7**, now an expensive dormitory for Hull commuters, is not only one of the most charming to be found along the Yorkshire Wolds Way but also has perhaps the greatest claim to fame. It was here in 1739 that the legendary highwayman, Dick Turpin, scourge of all coach travellers between London and York, was arrested.

The full story of how he came to be in this seemingly peaceful village can be learned in The Green Dragon Inn, Cowgate, which is as good an excuse to take refreshment as you will ever get. A copy of his record of arrest, to be found inside the pub, says that one John Palmer had stolen some horses in Lincolnshire and driven them across the Humber to sell them. He got drunk at The Green Dragon, shot a gamecock and was subsequently unmasked as the famous Turpin. He was tried at York Assizes and sent to the gallows.

A CIRCULAR WALK FROM BRANTINGHAM

6 miles (9.7 km)

This brief introduction to classic Yorkshire Wolds countryside begins at the duck pond, Brantingham **9,** one of the most picturesque villages in the area. Walk up the dale road towards All Saints' Church **10** and turn right over a stile a short distance before reaching the church. Walk uphill and at the lane turn left for 300 yards (275 metres). Turn right through a handgate, taking an obvious path through a long, narrow strip of woodland. Keep walking until you reach a forestry track, then turn right for a short distance before turning sharp left on a path that goes steeply downhill through the trees leading into the pleasant upper reaches of Elloughton Dale. The path now joins a minor road which you cross to follow the path climbing up through the woods. Towards the top, the path curves round to the left before arriving at a woodland crossroads. Go straight ahead here as the path now bears right through an attractive narrow

Walking the Yorkshire Wolds Way on a crisp winter's day. Brantingham Church lies in the valley below.

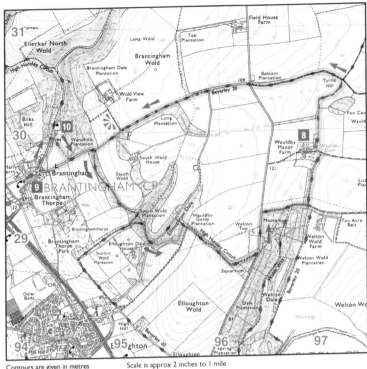

Contours are given in metres Scale is approx 2 inches to 1 mile
The vertical interval is 5m

belt of trees. On reaching the road, turn left past the riding centre at Welton Top. Turn right on the field path beside the access
road to Welton Wold Farm. A domed mausoleum can be seen
through the trees on the right (less visible with summer's
greenery). This is the tomb of the local Raikes family, built in
1818, but there is no public access. Turn left beside a long plantation of conifers to walk along the Yorkshire Wolds Way for
400 yards (365 metres) to Wauldby Manor Farm **8**, a splendid
late-Georgian farmhouse with a chapel built to serve the ham-
let of Wauldby. The dam has moorhens, coots and mallards.

Turn left at the top of the pond, then right past the farm cottages along a track that gently undulates to Turtle Hill, and left
again for a virtually straight 2-mile (3.2-km) walk. This takes you
along level or sloping tracks, a minor road, and one of the best-
preserved green lanes in the Wolds, back towards Brantingham.
At the end of Wandhills Plantation you can continue straight
down the hill into Brantingham or turn right to follow your out-
ward route to return to the village via the church.

Brantingham Church, centrepiece of a popular and picturesque dale.

2 South Cave to Goodmanham

past North Newbald
11 miles (17.7 km)

This stretch of the Yorkshire Wolds Way could easily be accomplished by four hours' solid tramping, but such an exercise would deprive the walker of the chance to explore some of the most interesting features to be found within easy reach of the route. Therefore, by all means permit yourself a late start but leave room for a look around South Cave, some minor off-path walking to such fascinating sights at Newbald's church, and a significant detour for those planning a night's stop at Market Weighton.

South Cave **13** was almost certainly inhabited during Roman times, lying as it did on the main road from Lincoln to York, but there are no surviving relics from this period. Unusually, there are two 'ends' to the village. The West End is centred around All Saints Church, a Victorian restoration of a medieval building, and it was here that the earliest settlement was established. Charters for markets and fairs were granted in 1291 and 1314, but in the Middle Ages the market moved half a mile eastwards to what is today's main village centre. The most interesting building is the Market Hall in (what else?) Market Place, a yellow-grey brick structure built in 1796. Up the hill is Cave Castle, a castellated Gothic house built in 1804 for the Barnards, wealthy Hull shipping merchants, but now converted into a hotel.

South Cave is mostly a dormitory for affluent Hull commuters, but it also has good accommodation and a couple of pubs, which make it a handy stop for Yorkshire Wolds Way walkers.

To rejoin the National Trail, walk back up the tarmac lane (signposted Riplingham) and just beyond the village find the path **A** leading to the left. This route ascends gently to Little Wold Plantation, where you turn right and walk alongside it for about half a mile (800 metres). This offers splendid views south across the Humber. When the path joins a track, turn right and descend the slope to Comber Dale, going left **B** down into one of the most serene parts of the walk. Just before the point where the path curves right into Weedley Dale is Weedley Springs, from which North Cave's stream rises.

Through the gate ahead **C** is a section of the dismantled Hull–Barnsley railway line **14**, which is followed for nearly half a mile (800 metres) and stops just short of the 2,116-yard (1,934-metre) Drewton Tunnel (now sealed). Take the steps leading up the steep embankment on the left and follow the path into West Hill Plantation and the lovely East Dale. At the head of the dale, the path arrives at a stile. This marks the end of the path's route across the wooded slopes of the Southern Wolds. From here, the Yorkshire Wolds Way crosses wide expanses of chalk tops and follows deep, mainly grassy, dry valleys.

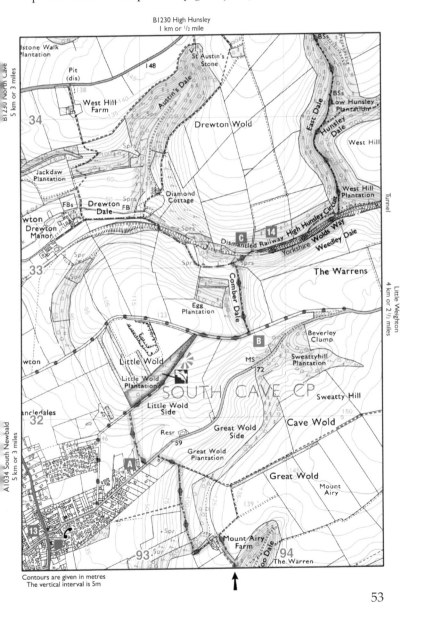

Contours are given in metres
The vertical interval is 5m

Only a short distance off the National Trail, North Newbald is well worth a detour fo

...nan church, village green and two excellent pubs!

Turn left and follow the field edge round to the B1230 **D**. Turn right towards the beacon, taking care on this busy road, then left onto another field path. The radio mast that you can see is at High Hunsley and transmits radio and television programmes to the area. Turn right along the minor road, continue ahead over the crossroads then left again **E** to follow the field path down into Swin Dale. The dew pond **15** is of the modern type: concrete-lined rather than built on a man-made saucer of mud or clay as was the practice of Anglo-Danish settlers.

Walkers wishing to make a detour to North Newbald should fork left **F** at the end of the dale on a path that joins a metalled road for half a mile and leads into the village.

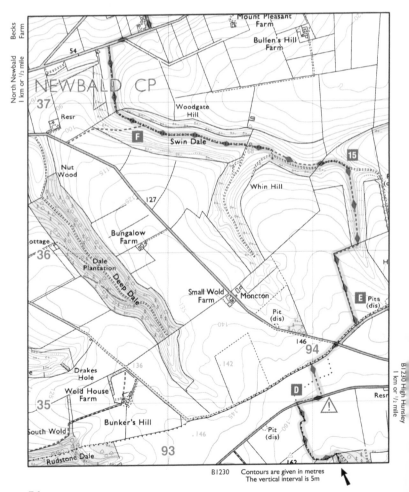

B1230   Contours are given in metres
The vertical interval is 5m

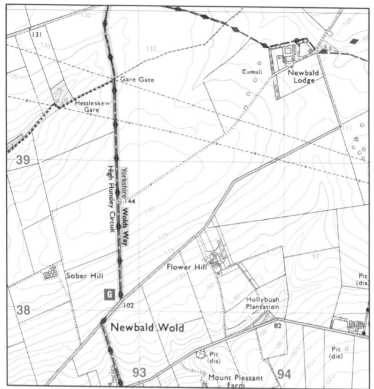

Contours are given in metres
The vertical interval is 5m

The most interesting feature is its famous cruciform St Nicholas Church, said to be the finest Norman church in the East Riding. It was built around 1140 and has been exceptionally well preserved. Newbald also has a classic village green, two good pubs and the timeless atmosphere of an English village, the like of which you will not find further north on this walk. If walking from South Cave, it makes an excellent lunch stop.

The quickest way back to the National Trail is to leave the village by the lane that passes the school and Becks Farm, then take the road on the left and rejoin the footpath at a signpost pointing left along the Gare Gate track.

Walkers who did not make the detour to North Newbald should have continued ahead at the top of Swin Dale, turning right on the road, left on a track past a small farm, right on a minor road, and left again **G** on the farm track to Gare Gate. The path stretches in a straight line now for about 2 ¹/₂ miles (3.6 km), joining the

Sancton–Arras road as it passes Hessleskew Farm **16**. Just before the farm across the field on the right (no public access) is a group of trees marking the spot of what was a Roman amphitheatre.

Although there are few clearly visible reminders – mainly some barrows and tumuli in fields that are inaccessible to the walker – this part of the Wolds was one of the greatest settlements of the Parisii, late-Iron Age warriors. A square cemetery containing chariots, horse harnesses, skeletons of ponies, bronze brooches, armlets and beads was found a short distance down the Beverley–Market Weighton road.

Cross the busy A1079 with care, follow the farm road **H** and pass between the buildings at Arras, and follow a hedge out into open countryside again. This path eventually descends into a valley known as the Market Weighton Gap, through

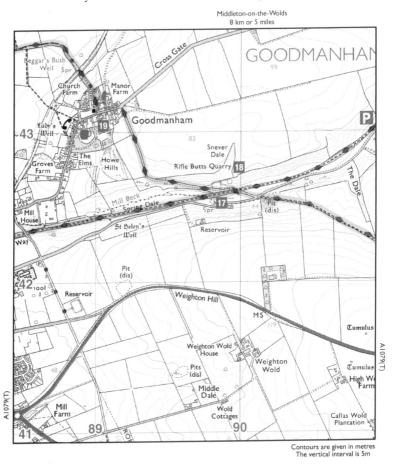

Middleton-on-the-Wolds
8 km or 5 miles

Contours are given in metres
The vertical interval is 5m

which the North Eastern Railway constructed a line **17** between Beverley and Market Weighton in 1865. This is now a bridleway and footpath known as the Hudson Way, named after the great railway builder, George Hudson.

Rifle Butts Quarry **18** is a nationally important geological reserve managed by the Yorkshire Wildlife Trust. The quarry face shows a section of Red and White Chalk overlying Lias strata; hundreds of metres of intervening rocks are 'missing'!

Walkers have a choice to make here: whether to spend the night at Market Weighton or walk on to Goodmanham. Walkers continuing along the Yorkshire Wolds Way to Goodmanham should follow the signposts away from the railway line, northwards on the metalled lane into the village, turning left on to the main village street. The 'finishing post' of this particular section of the National Trail is the small village church **19**. Those pausing in Goodmanham (see page 64) for refreshments may wish to walk a short distance further down the hill from the church (off the Yorkshire Wolds Way) to the Goodmanham Arms.

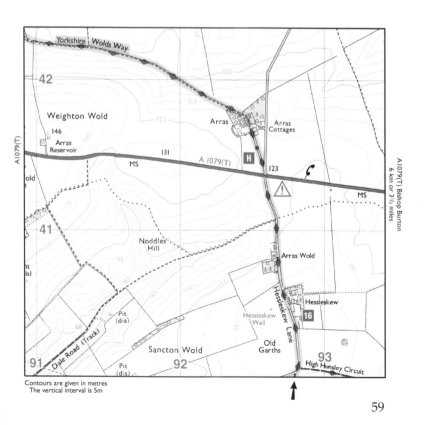

Contours are given in metres
The vertical interval is 5m

If you are intending to stay in Market Weighton: from the Market Weighton Gap it is an easy walk along the course of the former Beverley–Market Weighton railway line **17** into town. For most of the route, there are high embankments on either side, piled with hawthorn entangled with brambles and nettles. The walker's attention will be diverted by finches, tits and members of the thrush family, in autumn including fieldfare and redwing, which feast off the berries.

As the line reaches the built-up area, another railway joins from the right: it once linked Market Weighton with Driffield. At the end of a development of modern houses **I**, continue straight on and you will quickly be in the town's main street **20** (see below).

The route back to the Yorkshire Wolds Way is found by walking along the York Road from the centre, through a handgate **J** to the right beyond the new housing development, and following a rough path over a field to its left-hand corner. Continue in a straight line through several fields known as Weighton Clay Field, cross the road and pass through Towthorpe Grange Farm. Go through the gate and keep to the track which, shortly, joins a road for a brief distance before turning right through the gates of Londesborough Park **21**. The Yorkshire Wolds Way is rejoined beyond the lake, just before the track enters the village of Londesborough.

Market Weighton

Once the busiest rail junction in the East Riding, outside Hull, with four lines meeting at its now demolished station, as well as an important crossroads of five main roads, Market Weighton **20** was an extremely busy place until the 1960s. It appeared in *Domesday* as *Wicstun* and received a market charter in 1251, but it was mainly a small village built around All Saints Parish Church, which was begun in the 11th century.

The village became a town as a result of the construction of the Market Weighton Canal in 1772, an 11-mile (18-km) waterway to the Humber on which was carried much of the East Riding's agricultural produce and quarried chalk. It closed in 1900.

John Wesley preached at the Methodist church in Market Place, but perhaps the town's greatest claim to fame was the Yorkshire Giant, William Bradley, who was born here in 1787. He matured to a height of 7ft 9in (2.36 metres), weighed 27 stone (172 kg) and became a celebrated fairground attraction

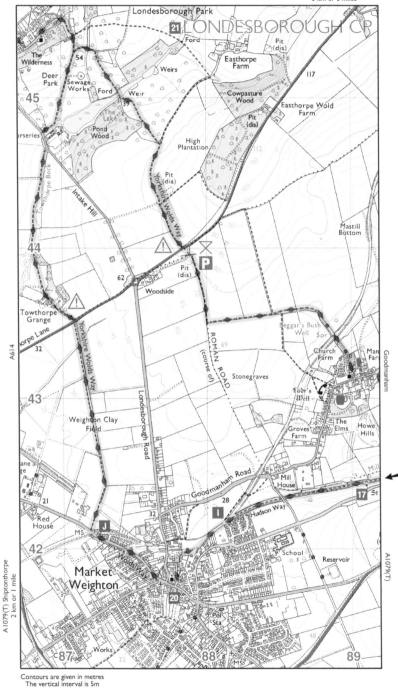

Londesborough Park

21 LONDESBOROUGH CP

Ford

The Wilderness

54

Easthorpe Farm

Pit (dis)

117

Deer Park

Weirs

Sewage Works

Ford

Weir

Cowpasture Wood

Easthorpe Wold Farm

45

39

The Lake

Pond Wood

High Plantation

Pit (dis)

112

110

rseries

Pit (dis)

Yorkshire Wolds Way

105

100

Intake Hill

Towthorpe Beck

95

Mastill Bottom

44

⚠

☓

P

62

Pit (dis)

Woodside

Beggar's Bush Well Spr

Towthorpe Grange

⚠

orpe Lane

Yorkshire Wolds Way

32

ROMAN ROAD (course of)

69

Church Farm

Man Far

Goodmanham

A614

Stonegraves

43

Lady's Well

Londesborough Road

Weighton Clay Field

Groves Farm

The Elms

Howe Hills

ane ge

21

Goodmanham Road

Mill House

Red House

MS

J

Hudson Way

17 St

←

28

1

42

32

School

Reservoir

A1079(T)

Market Weighton

Wolds Way

20

A1079(T) Shipton thorpe 2 km or 1 mile

Pol Sta

48

C87

22

Works

88

MS

89

Contours are given in metres
The vertical interval is 5m

61

THE
MARKET WEIGHTON
GIANT

THE FOOTPRINT
OF
WILLIAM BRADLEY
THE TALLEST
ENGLISHMAN EVER
RECORDED WHO LIVED
IN THIS HOUSE
BORN 10 FEB 1787
DIED 30 MAY 1820
HEIGHT 7FT 9INS
WEIGHT 27 STONES

ERECTED BY
MARKET WEIGHTON
CIVIC TRUST

In a giant's footstep: William Bradley's amazing boot print on a wall at Market Weighton

throughout England until his death, due to consumption, at the age of 33. You can see a memorial tablet marking his grave *inside* the parish church – it was feared that grave robbers would steal his remarkable corpse if it was buried in the churchyard. There is also a tablet on the wall of his birthplace (at the top of Linegate) showing the precise size of Bradley's boot. The doorway of the house was specially constructed to take his great bulk.

Old railway lines

On this stretch of the Yorkshire Wolds Way walkers encounter three disused railway lines, indicating that prior to the cuts of the 1960s the area was well served by connections through to the industrial West Riding.

The Hull–Barnsley Railway **14**, followed for a short distance in Weedley Dale, has the most interesting history of the three. It linked Alexandra Dock in Hull with the Yorkshire coalfields and was a direct challenge to a line already operated by the North Eastern Railway. The new line took a workforce of 4,900 men to build and opened for business on 20th July 1885 but, while coal exports via the line soon quadrupled, the competing company lowered its charges and the new line encountered severe financial difficulties. Inevitably, the two merged in 1922. Most of the line is private with no rights-of-way along it.

The Market Weighton–Beverley line **17** was opened by the North Eastern Railway on 1st May 1865, running through a natural valley known as the Market Weighton Gap. Its last train ran on 29th November 1965. The line was lifted and today it is a walkers' footpath known as the Hudson Way, named after George Hudson, the 'Railway King' (see page 92), who had fallen from grace by the time of the line's construction. It joins the town with Cherry Burton and will be used by Yorkshire Wolds Way walkers planning a stop at Market Weighton for accommodation. It also forms part of the excellent circular walk from Goodmanham. It is owned and managed by East Riding of Yorkshire Council.

The Market Weighton–Driffield line **24** (see pages 69 and 71) is seen at Goodmanham and Enthorpe. The line's construction was quite recent, opening on 18th April 1890. Originally there were plans to link it with the Hull–Barnsley line but its main traffic was passenger trains carrying West Riding families to the seaside at Bridlington. It was closed in August 1965 and is now in private ownership.

Kiplingcotes Derby

One of the most historic features to be found in the Yorkshire Wolds is the Kiplingcotes Racecourse, home of England's oldest horse race. Although not on the route of the Yorkshire Wolds Way itself, the entire length of the 4-mile (6.4-km) track, covering a rough green lane that has been partly tarmacked on its final section, is included in the excellent circular walk from Goodmanham (see page 69).

The date of the first race, as painted on the winning post **23** (see pages 69 and 70), is 1519, but the earliest actual record of the race was not until 1555. The Kiplingcotes Derby is still run every year on the third Thursday of March, for prize money that is less than £100, being the interest on an endowment provided by 'five noblemen, 19 baronets and 25 gentlemen' in the 17th century.

By horse racing standards, the Derby is a pretty inelegant affair, with spectators apt to end up with a fair splattering of mud. Most competitors are amateur riders, often from the local farming community. The rules state that horses must be able to 'convey horsemen's weight ten stones, exclusive of saddle, to enter at ye post eleven o'clock on the morning of ye race. The race to be run before two.' The most interesting feature of the Derby is that the person coming second receives more than the winner. He or she gets the entrance money, whereas the victor gets only the interest on the original sum.

Goodmanham

It is difficult to believe that this sleepy village was the scene of a crucial event in the coming of Christianity to Britain. A heathen temple stood on the site now occupied by the little Norman church when, in AD 626, Edwin, the Saxon King of Northumbria, was converted to the Christian faith by Paulinus, the great missionary. Edwin, led by his High Priest, Coifi, then set about desecrating the temple. The Venerable Bede described 'Goodmundingaham', as it was then called, as 'this one-time place of idols'.

Nothing of the temple remains today, but the church **19**, in the centre of this spread-out village, is now most notable for its highly decorative 15th-century font, perhaps the most outstanding in the Wolds. It stands on a short stem and is 5 feet (1.5 metres) high with rich carving over the bowl's eight sides.

Oilseed rape

The most dramatic feature on the landscape of the Yorkshire Wolds is undoubtedly the great yellow sheets of oilseed rape that flare all along the footpath in spring and early summer.

Open to riders, all breeds and all ages, astride or side-saddle and wearing whatever you wish, the Kiplingcotes Derby is not run under Jockey Cub rules!

The crop is one of the *Brassica* family, which includes cabbage, swede and mustard, and it originated in the Mediterranean region. It first became a popular English crop in the south in the early 1970s and slowly worked its way north, its popularity increasing roughly at the same rate as concern

All Saints Church, Goodmanham, built on a site once occupied by a pagan temple.

that high consumption of cholesterol and saturated fats was linked with heart disease.

As the name implies, the crop is grown for its seeds, which do not ripen until late in the season, so it is harvested in August and September. The oil is extracted for use in margarines and cooking oils, and a great deal of the latter is exported from Britain to the Middle and Far East. The remaining vegetable matter is processed for cattle feed.

As demand for unsaturated fat products has grown, so has the number of fields blazing yellow as far as the eye can see from April to July. Wolds farmers have also found that oilseed rape is a useful 'break crop', when grown in soil that has been planted with cereals like wheat and barley for several successive years. This breaks the cycle of infection by diseases that afflict cereals.

There have been two side-effects of this greatly increased production. One is the growth in bee population – the brilliant yellow flowers contain good nectar for the worker-bees to collect. The other is the dramatic rise of the pollen count – the crop is blamed for increased misery for thousands of hay-fever sufferers.

A CIRCULAR WALK FROM GOODMANHAM

13 miles (21 km)

This excellent route makes a fine introduction to the Yorkshire Wolds, taking in as it does so many of the landscape's classic features, such as the peaceful chalk downs, the quiet Wolds lanes, an unspoilt village, disused railway lines and the historic Kiplingcotes Racecourse. Although quite a lot of this walk follows country roads, traffic is very light and there are wide grass verges which make for safe and softer walking

Begin from Goodmanham Church **19** and follow the Yorkshire Wolds Way down the hill and all the way to Londesborough village. Pass the church **22**, turn right and at the road junction leave the Yorkshire Wolds Way and turn up the road signposted to Nunburnholme and Warter. Before you turn right at the next crossroads, pause to admire the extensive views. On a clear day you can see the White Horse of Kilburn on the edge of the North York Moors, York Minster, The Pennines, numerous power stations and the chimneys of Scunthorpe. As you continue your walk there are also pleasant views down to the right over forest and field.

After almost 2 miles (3.2 km) turn sharp right down a narrow strip of tarmac bordered by wide grass verges indicating the course of an ancient green road. At the brow of the next rise you will pass the winning post **23** for the famous Kiplingcotes Derby (see page 63), England's oldest horse race. Cross the busy A163 Bridlington road and continue ahead for about three-quarters of a mile (1.2 km) along the course of the race track to Enthorpe Wood. The track narrows here and joins a metalled farm road. Go over the bridge at Enthorpe Cutting to cross the disused Market Weighton–Driffield railway line **24**, continue ahead along the county road and after about 1 mile (1.6 km) turn right at the crossroads. At the bottom of the hill go forward-right up the lane to Kiplingcotes Station **25** on the old Market Weighton–Beverley railway line **17**, now part of the Hudson Way.

The path passes the Yorkshire Wildlife Trust reserve at Kiplingcotes Chalk Pit where over 500 species of plants and animals have been recorded and then joins the Yorkshire Wolds Way near Rifle Butts Quarry, another YWT reserve famous for its unique geological exposure. Follow the road back into Goodmanham.

(for map see pages 70–1)

Scale is approx 2 inches to 1 mile

Contours are given in metres
The vertical interval is 5m

70

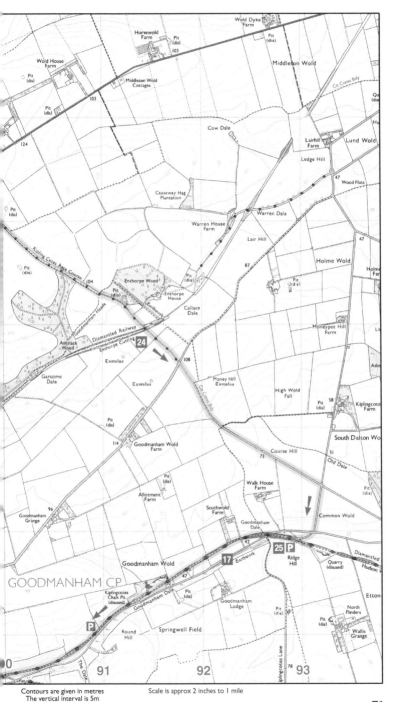

Contours are given in metres
The vertical interval is 5m

Scale is approx 2 inches to 1 mile

71

3 Goodmanham to Thixendale

through Londesborough and Fridaythorpe
20 miles (32.2 km)

This section of the Yorkshire Wolds Way is the longest described here. However, it could easily be broken into two shorter stages. For instance, the overnight stop could be at Millington, a fairly effortless 8-mile (13-km) walk from Goodmanham. This would provide an opportunity to explore the nearby Millington Pasture and Millington Wood (see pages 78 and 93), both of which do not lie on the footpath. Alternatively, the walker could continue to Huggate, a more demanding 13 miles (21 km) from Goodmanham, and find overnight accommodation there. This would permit a shorter walk the following day on the 7-mile (11.2-km) stretch to Thixendale, along some classic dry valleys that certainly repay being savoured at leisure.

The path resumes from Goodmanham Church **19**. Turn right down the hill, and join the clear dirt track as it goes under the bridge that once carried the Market Weighton–Driffield railway line. Follow the rutted track straight on, curving round the field edge and keeping a drainage ditch on your left. The path swings round to the right, straightens out and emerges at the top of a very large picnic area beside the main A163 road, which connects the cities of West Yorkshire with the popular seaside resort of Bridlington. There are timber tables and benches at which to enjoy a break, if you wish, but Yorkshire Wolds Way walkers will soon have a choice of infinitely more peaceful picnic sites as the path traverses Londesborough Park **21**.

Cross the road with care, and join a track – actually part of the Malton to Brough Roman road – through a field, keeping the hedge to your left. The fertile Vale of York spreads out flatly to the west and ahead lie the red roofs of Londesborough. This track links with a metalled road coming up from the left and proceeds forward into the Londesborough Estate. At the landmark circle of six huge horse chestnut trees, fork left **A** over a stile and go down the gentle slope, fording the stream by a plank bridge. The stream issues into the artificially created Londesborough Lake, part of the Park **21** laid out by the third Earl of Burlington in the 17th–18th century. The original Hall was demolished in 1819, its materials used for an addition to Chatsworth, and was replaced by today's red brick structure,

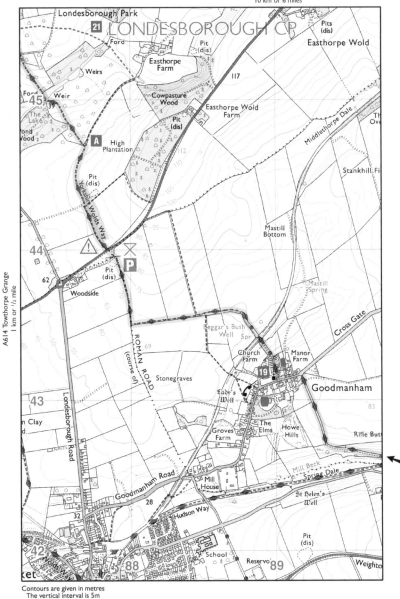

Contours are given in metres
The vertical interval is 5m

seen in the distance through the trees. There are, however, some remnants of the earlier house still visible, notably a stepped terrace, two large pedestals, some gatepiers and some smaller pedestals dating from the 17th century.

Electric sunset: the huge Drax power station, seen in the distance from above Londesboro

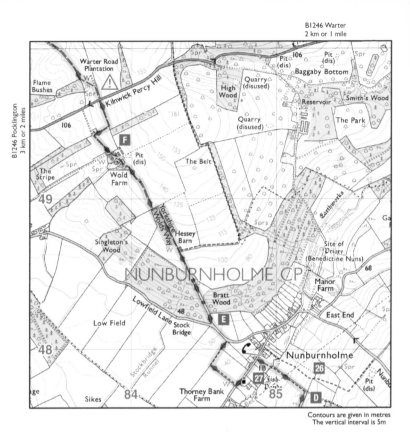

Contours are given in metres
The vertical interval is 5m

Up the hill, join a track that merges from the left **B**, a section of the Yorkshire Wolds Way for those walkers who chose to stop at Market Weighton. Pass through a gate and walk along the track that curves up the hill to the left, through the trees, to emerge on a village street in Londesborough. All Saints Church **22** is worth a brief detour, it has a sundial and 11th-century Anglo-Danish cross above its Norman south door. Near the church is a panel giving information about this interesting village and estate. Beyond the church, turn right uphill and at the cross-roads continue straight ahead along the minor road for about a mile (1.6 km) There are excellent views westwards from here over the Vale of York. Turn right at the T-junction **C** then left through the farmyard of Partridge Hall. Continue straight ahead over the field passing Thorns Wood on your left. Go through the kissing-gate from near which there are fine views over the village of Nunburnholme **26** and proceed ahead, keeping a fence on your right. Follow the field edge round **D**, dropping down to a footbridge over Nunburnholme Beck and through a small field to a road. The Yorkshire Wolds Way turns left towards the church **27**, where the eminent Victorian ornithologist, Francis Orpen Morris (see page 92), was rector from 1854 until 1893. The Revd Morris supported the Association for the Protection of Seabirds founded in Bridlington in 1868 which was instrumental in the passing of early legislation to protect wild birds. It is worth entering the church to see the fine Anglo-Saxon cross.

Turn right off the road and follow the field edges on to another road. Continue up the slope, and fork right **E** on the track through Bratt Wood. Cross a field, then go over a stile to another field and a track serving Wold Farm. At the farm **F** bear left down a limestone track to join a metalled lane and continue ahead for about 100 yards (91 metres). Turn sharp right by the house, go up the field and turn left to join the road which links Pocklington with Warter. Cross the road and follow the path leading to the top of the plantation ahead.

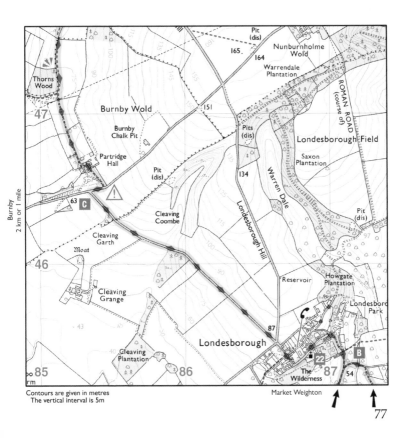

Go through a handgate and continue ahead, passing through Low Warrendale Farm and on to join the road at a right-angle bend **G.** The Yorkshire Wolds Way now turns right up the hillside to begin one of the most memorable sections on the whole of the route. Behind are fine long distance views to the west. The flat Vale of York floor has three sets of power station cooling towers: Drax to the left, Eggborough in the middle, and Ferrybridge to the right.

At the end of the plantation, turn sharp left to cross the field, then left again **H** to reach the edge of the hillside overlooking Millington **28**. On a clear day the views are extensive. The line of the Pennine Hills is clearly visible. The towers of York Minster can be seen, as can the edge of the North York Moors near Sutton Bank. Look very carefully and you may even see the White Horse of Kilburn, a huge turf-cut figure on the hillside above the village of Kilburn.

Below is a bird's-eye view of Millington nestling at the foot of the chalk escarpment. The small fields divided by ancient hedges are very striking and indicate what so much of the Wolds landscape must have looked like after the Enclosure Acts of the 18th/19th century had been implemented. Turn right along the edge of the hill which constitutes a magnificent promenade overlooking one of the least spoilt of the Wolds' dales.

The Way passes to the right of Warren Farm and after a short dog-leg continues ahead with the hedge on the right. Opposite is Millington Wood, and north of that can be seen the slopes of Millington Pasture **29**. Where the path overlooks Sylvan Dale **I,** swing down to the left to cross a stile and then steeply down to the valley floor. The name 'Sylvan Dale' suggests a time when this and other Wolds valleys were more heavily tree covered. Today, the scrub-covered slopes remain largely untouched by plough or fertiliser and often accommodate a wide range of wild flowers with their attendant butterflies and birds.

When you reach the valley floor the path strikes steeply straight up the opposite side to a stile and then continues ahead along the field edge. On the left can be seen the line of a substantial earthwork **30** which was constructed by the La Tene tribesmen in the late Iron Age.

Follow the hedge and earthwork where they descend left **J** down into Nettle Dale before climbing again up the opposite slope for a short distance before bearing right **K** on a more gradual slope towards Jessop's Plantation.

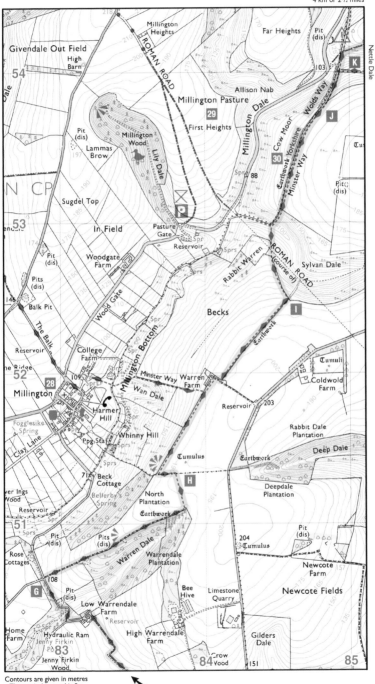

Huggate
4 km or 2¹/₂ miles

Givendale Out Field

Millington Heights

Far Heights

Pit (dis)

K

Nettle Dale

High Barn

54

103

ROMAN ROAD

Allison Nab

Millington Pasture

29

Wolds Way

J

First Heights

Cow Moor

30

Earthwork Yorkshire

Minster Way

Pit (dis)

Pit (dis)

Millington Wood

Lammas Brow

Lily Dale

Millington Dale

88

Spr

N CP

Sugdel Top

In Field

X

P

Pasture Gate

Spr

Reservoir

Sprs

ROMAN ROAD (course of)

Sylvan Dale

53

Woodgate Farm

Rabbit Warren

Pit (dis)

Spr

Pits (dis)

146

Balk Pit

Wood Gate

Sprs

Becks

Earthwork

I

The Balk

Reservoir

College Farm

Spr

Millington Bottom

Spr

Tumuli

Coldwold Farm

e Ridge

52

28

109

Minster Way

Warren Farm

Millington

Harmer Hill

Wan Dale

Reservoir

203

Rabbit Dale Plantation

Deep Dale

Fogglesike Spring

Whinny Hill

Ppg Sta

Sprs

Earthwork

Clay Lane

Tumulus

Deepdale Plantation

71

Beck Cottage

Bellerby's Spring

North Plantation

H

er Ings Wood

Reservoir

51

Earthwork

Sprs

Pit (dis)

Pits (dis)

Warren Dale

204

Tumulus

Pit (dis)

Rose Cottages

Warrendale Plantation

Newcote Farm

108

Pit (dis)

Bee Hive

Limestone Quarry

Newcote Fields

G

Low Warrendale Farm

Reservoir

Home Farm

Hydraulic Ram

Jenny Firkin

83

High Warrendale Farm

Gilders Dale

85

Jenny Firkin Wood

84

Crow Wood

151

Contours are given in metres
The vertical interval is 5m

79

Walk around the edge of the plantation and turn right **L** across Huggate Sheepwalk, above Pasture Dale, to a road. Walk along this to the junction, where you follow the signs across the road. From here, when visibility is perfect, it is possible to see as far away as Lincoln Cathedral, the towers of the Humber Bridge and Sheffield in the south, York Minster to the west, and the lighthouse on Flamborough Head to the east.

Cross York Lane **M** and follow the farm road, passing Glebe Farm. On the hillside ahead you can see a diamond-shaped plantation. Larch was planted here to celebrate Queen Victoria's Diamond Jubilee in 1897, but the plantation was felled for mine props during the Second World War and an assortment of trees and bushes grew in their place, preserving, to some extent, the original diamond motif on the hillside.

When you reach the road junction, the Yorkshire Wolds Way turns left **N** but those who intend to spend the night at the village of Huggate **31**, or who simply wish to use its facilities, will turn right. At the centre is a large village green and a pond

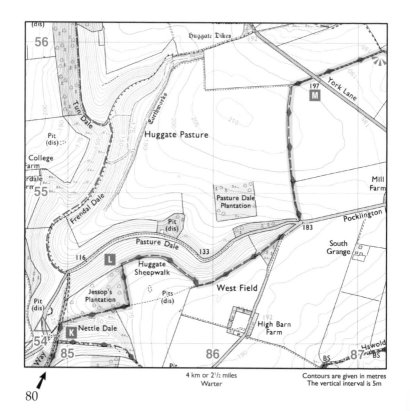

4 km or 2¹/₂ miles
Warter

Contours are given in metres
The vertical interval is 5m

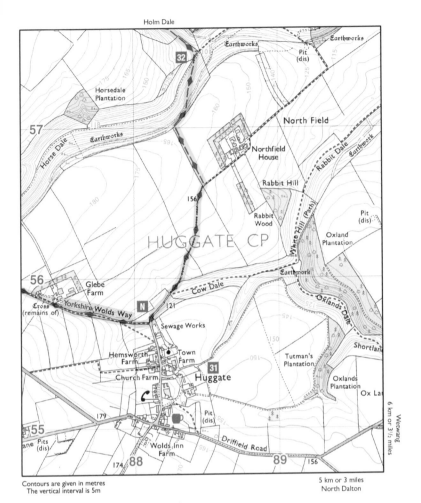

Contours are given in metres
The vertical interval is 5m

5 km or 3 miles
North Dalton

on one of the few natural clay basins to have formed above the chalk. St Mary's Church has the locally rare feature of a spire on its 14th-century tower. The village is notorious for being cut off for several days at a time after winter snowstorms, since all approach roads involve steep inclines and exposed stretches that suffer from extensive drifting.

If you choose to walk on to Thixendale, follow the track along the sides of some fairly exposed fields, descend gradually into Horse Dale and, at the bottom, curve to the left up the classic chalk valley of Holm Dale. Near the junction of the two dales **32** is the site of one of the many medieval villages wiped out at the time of the Black Death.

The striking spire on the 14-century tower of St Mary's Church at Huggate is a domin

...re of the local landscape.

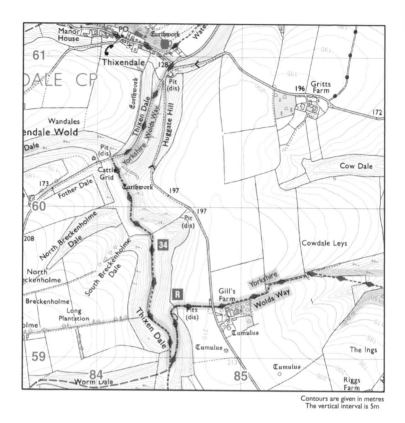

Contours are given in metres
The vertical interval is 5m

The path reaches the dale head and you proceed through a gate near two distinctive horse chestnut trees on a track that emerges on the main street **O** of Fridaythorpe **33**. Turn right and then left on the road signposted to Thixendale. On the left, past the Manor House Restaurant, is a wooden sign commemorating the 21st anniversary of the Yorkshire Wolds Way on Thursday 2nd October 2003. It records that Hessle Haven is 39 miles (63 km) away to the south and that Filey Cliffs are 40 miles (64 km) to the north, making Fridaythorpe the approximate halfway mark.

The village is one of the largest in the Wolds and, as the suffix 'thorpe' suggests, was established by Danish invaders. It is possible that the first half of the name was derived from the Norse goddess of love, Freya. Today's Fridaythorpe is a miscellany of 18th-, 19th- and 20th-century housing. St Mary's Church, behind a farm, is worth seeking out for its south doorway (*c.* 1120), which Pevsner described as 'utterly barbaric'. It has a jumble of columns, chip-carving, a rope motif, rosettes and decorated scallops.

Turn off the Thixendale Road on a track **P** just before the large modern mill. After following the edge of several fields the path turns right to descend, at an angle, into West Dale. Bear right at the bottom then left up a small tributary valley **Q** to join the road on the north side of Gill's Farm. Cross the road and after a short distance the route bends down into Thixen Dale **R**, regarded by some as one of the most enjoyable parts of the Yorkshire Wolds Way.

Follow the line of trees down the chalk valley **34**, pass through a gate, and then walk along a rutted track. Steep, uncultivated banks of grasses and wild flowers rise on either side. Skylarks and yellowhammers are everywhere in spring and summer, as are peacefully grazing lambs and sheep. Swing right on the tarmac lane and left into the main street of Thixendale. The inn is immediately on the right.

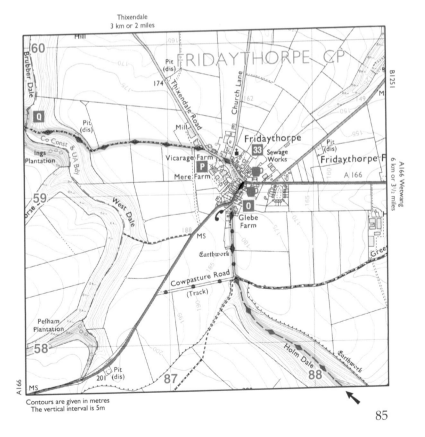

Contours are given in metres
The vertical interval is 5m

Sheep – once the principal shaper of the Wolds landscape – are seen here in Millington L

Sheep walks

Until cereal production was increased to feed an accelerating population in the 18th century, the Yorkshire Wolds were covered by sheep 'walks'. The conversion from very early crop-growing to stock-rearing in the Middle Ages contributed to the abandonment of many small villages, as sheep-rearing offered greatly reduced employment.

Most of the land seen on the tops today was at one time a vast, grassy sheep walk, but there are still some sections surviving – usually close to the steep banks that ploughs cannot reach.

One of the last surviving sheep walks was at Millington Pasture **29**, which was finally enclosed for cultivation in the 1960s.

Many of today's field boundaries follow the lines of ring-fences and ditches, used to keep flocks together, and this explains why some fields are positively vast.

Chalk banks

The plunging banks of the Yorkshire Wolds, seen in places like Millington Dale and at numerous points around Thixendale, form one of the few landscapes in Britain that have been pre-

Millington Springs, one of the rare stretches of water in the chalk Wolds.

served more or less intact for the best part of a thousand years. Woodland clearances from Neolithic times had steadily created a land suitable for cultivation, but the steep scarps were difficult to manage. The constant cropping of the grasses and seedlings by sheep and rabbits, introduced for their meat and fur, created and maintained the habitat still seen today.

The banks have been preserved and from the calcium-rich soil there springs a highly distinctive flora which, in turn, attracts a wide range of animal life. The major difference is that since the myxomatosis epidemic of the 1950s, which wiped out great numbers of rabbits, natural grazing has been reduced and tall grasses have thrived. There are still many species of wild flowers present in these banks in spring and summer, none more eye-catching from a distance than the cowslip, truly the flower of the Yorkshire Wolds. In some places, its spread actually inhibits the growth of other species. Look out, also, for salad burnet, rock rose, thyme, mouse-ear chickweed, mouse-ear hawkweed, fairy flax, pignut, sheep's fescue, eyebright, burnet saxifrage, harebell and dropwort.

Such a rich flora attracts equally distinctive butterflies, such as peacocks, marbled white, small copper, meadow brown and orange-tips.

Ponds and streams of the Wolds

Chalk is a highly porous rock and the lack of water supply has been a major factor in the Wolds' colonisation and development. Settlements were mainly situated on the site of springs, such as at Millington and Nunburnholme, but on the high Wolds Anglo-Danish settlers, who established villages like Huggate and Fridaythorpe, created artificial ponds by making an impervious saucer of clay to collect dew and rainwater. You can still see these ponds today as you pass through the villages.

One of the most fascinating features of the Wolds is a natural trough, known as the Great Wold Valley, through which 'flows' the Gypsey Race, an elusive stream. It rises just off the footpath, between Wharram le Street and Duggleby, and flows somewhat erratically south-eastwards to Bridlington. Its name almost certainly comes from 'gypa', which is Norse for a spring. It runs only when the water table in the chalk reservoirs reaches a certain height. Strangely, this is more likely to happen after a dry spell than following prolonged rain. A local superstition has it that when the Gypsey Race runs, famine is imminent. However, it seems to surface every few years but famine – so far – has not occurred.

A gateway into the Londesborough Estate.

90

Londesborough and the 'Railway King'

The Yorkshire Wolds Way passes through the great Londesborough Estate **21**. Although now said to be a shadow of its former glory, this is one of the most pleasant spots to be found along the footpath. The park itself is thought to have been the site of a Roman settlement called *Delgovita*, and a mansion was built here in the 16th century. Its most celebrated resident was George Hudson, the famous 'Railway King' of the 19th century.

Hudson started out as a draper and eventually went into partnership. In 1827, on the eve of the railway boom, he invested a £30,000 inheritance in railway shares and then helped to gain Parliamentary approval for the York and North Midlands Railway. Three times Lord Mayor of York, he made the city the railway capital of England and bought the Londesborough Estate for £470,000 in 1845 when he was at the height of his success, controlling more than 1,000 miles of railway. He even constructed his own private railway station for the estate, on the York–Market Weighton line, but it has now been demolished. Hudson's reputation was ruined in 1849 when he was accused of fraud in his operation of the Eastern Counties Railway.

Revd Francis Orpen Morris

Nunburnholme has one great claim to fame. The splendid cream-washed rectory, next to St James Church **27**, was the home of the great Victorian ornithologist, Francis Orpen Morris.

He became rector at Nunburnholme in 1854 when he was in the process of publishing the six-volume *A History of British Birds* and was already busy with a new three-volume work, *A Natural History of the Nests and Eggs of British Birds*. Morris was an acknowledged pioneer of nature conservation in Victorian times and campaigned for bird protection by writing numerous letters to *The Times*; a collection of these letters was published in 1880. He also wrote authoritative books on British moths as well as an encyclopaedic guide to great country houses in Britain and Ireland.

After nearly 40 years at Nunburnholme, Morris died in 1893 at the age of 82. He is buried next to the church door, and in his memory the church bell is inscribed: 'I will imitate your birds by singing.'

Millington Pasture

The steep-sided valley of Millington Dale has been a popular local beauty spot for decades and the classic chalk banks and tops of Millington Pasture **29** were, until the 1960s, uncultivated downland. Totalling over 400 acres (162 hectares) of close-cropped grass meadow, the Pasture was the last surviving example of the traditional way of open-pasture sheep grazing in the Wolds. It was divided among 108 local farmers, each one awarded a 'gait' or 'gate' comprising pasture for six sheep, or four sheep plus two lambs. (The Gate Inn at Millington, incidentally, was named after this practice.)

Despite a public outcry and mass rambles by local walkers, fences were erected along the narrow road running along the Dale bottom. This ended the hitherto unrestricted access, and some crops were sowed on the higher ground. Nevertheless, the Pasture is still one of the few parts of the Wolds to convey a sense of being in a natural landscape, and it can be enjoyed by walkers taking the circular route from Millington village (see page 94).

Millington Wood, one of the few remaining wooded dales in the Wolds, lies nearby. It is primarily a classic ancient ash woodland and, as such, is a Site of Special Scientific Interest. A path starts from a picnic site and car park and runs right through the woods, enabling you to enjoy a nature walk.

The site is managed by East Riding of Yorkshire Council.

A CIRCULAR WALK FROM MILLINGTON

7 ½ miles (12.1 km)

This walk combines one of the most memorable stretches of the Yorkshire Wolds Way with exploration of the scenic Millington Pasture and the nearby village. Although it includes some road walking, traffic is usually light and the views offer ample compensation. The route can be shortened at the bottom of Sylvan Dale by returning via the dale road, allowing a visit to the beautiful Millington Wood Nature Reserve *en route* (the path into the woods is a cul-de-sac).

Begin at the church, walk down into the village, turn right, go past The Gate Inn then left near the end of the village to follow the road up the hill. Turn sharp left to join the Yorkshire Wolds Way as it follows a stone track up the hillside. Follow the route all the way along the western edge of the Wolds overlooking Millington. At the bottom of Nettle Dale, bear left to join the metalled road to walk back towards the village through the long, dry valley passing Millington spring on the way.

Turn right on the bridleway immediately opposite a pond on a route locally known as Thieves' Sty, part of a Roman road across the Wolds. Continue up Millington Pasture **29**, past Millington

Winter sunshine near Millington.

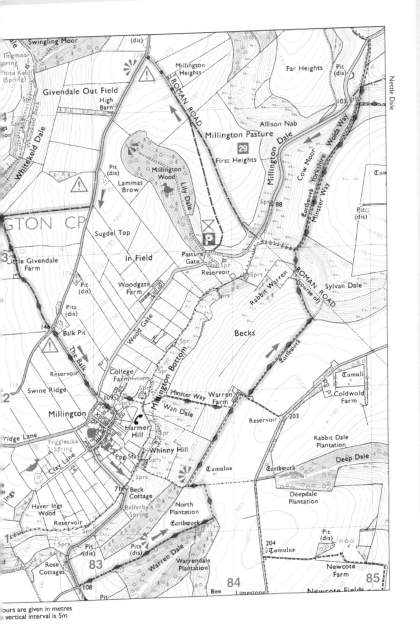

Contours are given in metres
the vertical interval is 5m

Heights Farm, then turn left on the county road. To avoid too much road walking turn right after about ³/₄ mile (1.2 km) down a bridleway then left to pass Little Givendale Farm. Cross the main road and return to Millington.

No water has flowed down these valleys for thousands of years, while today the chalk w

ily absorb all the rain that falls here.

4 Thixendale to Sherburn

via Wharram le Street and Wintringham
18 1/2 miles (29.8 km)

This section of the National Trail leads through some of the least-frequented countryside in the Wolds – the long northern scarp that rises above Wintringham – but also passes one of the most popular tourist 'honeypots' in the Yorkshire Wolds: the deserted medieval village of Wharram Percy.

There is no more tranquil village in the Yorkshire Wolds than Thixendale. Its mix of traditional and modern dwellings sits peacefully on either side of a single lane that hugs the floor of a straight chalk valley. Contours climb steeply all around, and the serene harmony of birdsong and sheep echoes over the pantile roofs throughout the spring and summer. The only way into the village is by narrow lanes or along footpaths through green dales that have stayed unchanged for centuries.

Six major dales clearly converge here but, with a bit of time studying a large-scale map, it is possible to trace a total of six-teen dales, like the spokes of a wheel, radiating out from the village. This may be the origin of the name 'Thixendale'.

The village has some useful facilities – a post office which is also a shop, a second shop and an excellent village pub, The Cross Keys. Thixendale was once served by the church at Wharram Percy but, when that was abandoned, there was no longer a place of worship. St Mary's Church was not built until 1870 and was the work of the Wolds church architect and restorer G. E. Street, paid for by the second Sir Tatton Sykes of Sledmere. He also provided the excellent lychgate, vicarage and school, the latter now used as a village hall.

To continue on the Yorkshire Wolds Way, leave Thixendale at the northern end of the main street **A**, by walking up a track that cuts up the hillside at an angle. Pass Cow Wold Barn on the right, cross the stile and keep to the track as it proceeds along the field edge. The change from the picturesque valley you have just left could not be more dramatic; the terrain here is of open fields, with buildings and hedges at a premium.

Descend briefly into Vessey Pasture Dale **B** and continue up the opposite bank, through a dale offshoot and along the line of an ancient earthwork, turning right **C** on a fine green road that stretches ahead in a straight line for 1 1/2 miles (2.5 km). At over 700 ft (215 metres), this is the highest point on the Way.

Thixendale, favourite of all villages for many Yorkshire Wolds Way walkers, nestles snugly in its valley.

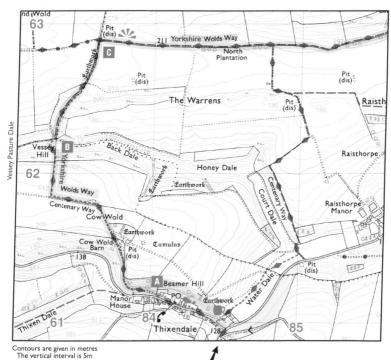

Contours are given in metres
The vertical interval is 5m

The fields here are almost prairie-like and it is tempting to assume that modern farming practices have grubbed out hedges to create bigger cereal crops but, in fact, medieval maps show that the field boundaries have not changed for centuries.

At the eastern end of North Plantation **D** turn left to follow the gradually sloping path down to Wharram Percy **35**, the deserted medieval settlement situated in one of the most beautiful and peaceful valleys you will find in the Yorkshire Wolds. On a fine, warm day you will be tempted to tarry longer than you planned but when you finally have to leave, take the path past the ruined church down to the old railway track **E**. Close by is the 1,734-yard (1,585-metre)-long Burdale Tunnel **36**, the longest railway tunnel in the Wolds. It was part of the Malton–Driffield railway line, which was opened in 1853 but closed in 1958. For decades it was the main link to the outside world for many Wolds residents and carried thousands of tons of chalk from the nearby Wharram (also known as Burdale) Quarry, which is now a Yorkshire Wildlife Trust Reserve famous for its orchids and butterflies.

The path crosses the railway trackbed and climbs gradually up to a small car park. Turn left down the road past Bella Farm **37** and where the road turns sharp right, continue ahead down the field side and then turn right into the sleepy village of Wharram le Street. St Mary's Church **38** has an Anglo-Saxon nave and west doorway and a Norman tower, but there is little else of interest here.

However, a mile (1.6 km) ahead at the crossroads lies Duggleby, to which the energetic can detour to see the famous Duggleby Howe, a huge round barrow, 20 ft (6 metres) high and 120 ft (37 metres) in diameter, where the remains of 50 late-Neolithic cremations were found, plus an assortment of flint arrowheads, tools carved from boars' and beavers' teeth, and bone pins. It lies 200 yards (185 metres) south of Duggleby Church, just off the B1253.

On the main street of Wharram le Street, turn left and at the end of the village go right **F** on the bridleway that begins up the hillside.

As the route gradually climbs, extensive views open up to the north and west. Beyond the market town of Malton may be seen the Howardian Hills, separated from the moors by the Coxwold–Gilling Gap. To the north, across the flat Vale of Pickering, rise the slopes of the North York Moors.

B1253

Duggleby

158

Pit
(dis)

Home
Farm

Spr

The Crofts

West End
Farm

Dogstoop
Plantation

Spr

Pits
(dis)

67

Spr

Broad Balk

145

Wandal

Cow Cliff

136

140

Boyes'
Plantation

135

122

Keeper's
Cottage

125

F

Wharram le Street

Oakhill
Springs

The Ings

Red House
Farm

Manor
Farm

128

120

66

Spr

38

140

Oak
Hill

am Grange
Farm

The Old
Vicarage

150

Centenary Way

160

Station Road

146

Reservoir

173

Quarry
(disused)

Station
House

175

58
65

180

Pit
(dis)

Wold Farm

Wold
Plantation

The Ings

WHARRAM CP

180

White
Hill

Centenary Way

Bella
Farm

35

Yorkshire Wolds Way

37

201

Medieval Village of
Wharram Percy
(site of)

E

36

P

Bella

Wharram
Percy

Church
(rems of)

Air
Shaft

Pit
(dis)

64

Spr

Wharram Percy Wold

Centenary Way

Drue Dale

208

212

Burdale Tunnel

210

Deep Dale

Air
Shaft

Pit
(dis)

Tumulus

Cattle
Grid

Air
Shaft

Fairy
Stones

Fairy Dale

209

205

Burdale N
Wold

D

Earthworks

159

Burdale Warren

63

86

87

North
Plantation

Kirk Hill

Burdale Quarry

Contours are given in metres
The vertical interval is 5m

B1248 North Grimston
2 km or 1 mile

B1248

Duggleby Dale

101

In spite of modern agricultural improvements, wild poppies still find a foothold in man

...ds fields and hedges.

Cross the B1253 and keep straight ahead along the field edge on a track, turning left at a barn and continuing west as the path slopes down to a footbridge across Whitestone Beck. Go straight uphill and turn right along the farm road **G**, following it past Wood House and on towards Settrington Wood. Do not enter the wood but bear right along its edge. Where Wold Barn once stood **H**, the path turns sharp left and then right to proceed northwards again, this time giving views to the west. This is enjoyable walking and the woods are good for spring flowers.

Cross the road **I** into a small plantation that surrounds Beacon Wold, a service reservoir collecting water from a bore-hole into the chalk. The triangulation pillar on the left is on the 650-ft (198-metre) contour. Proceed through the wood on a path that forms a verdant tunnel in spring and summer as it curves to right and left. When you arrive at a gate, one of the most memorable views on the entire Yorkshire Wolds Way will be revealed. The escarpment tumbles down to Wintringham and the Vale of Pickering is a patchwork of different shades of greens, browns and – when the oilseed rape is in season – yellows. The northern horizon is filled with the lumpy bulk of the North York Moors.

From Settrington the long-distance views stretch right across to the North York Moors.

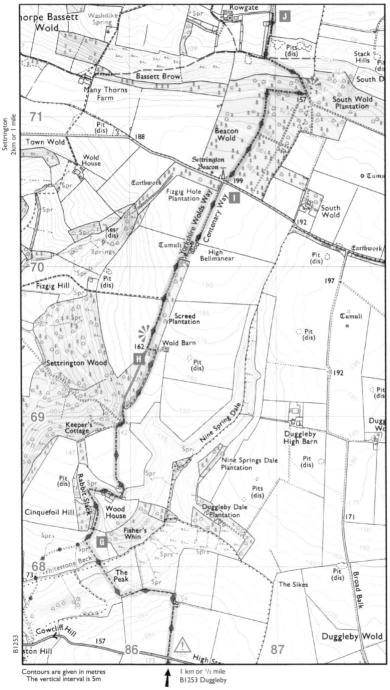

Settrington
2km or 1 mile

71

70

69

68

B1253

Thorpe Bassett Wold

Washdike Spring

Rowgate

J

Pits (dis)

Stack Hills

Bassett Brow

South D

Many Thorns Farm

South Wold Plantation

157

Pit (dis)

188

Beacon Wold

Town Wold

Wold House

Settrington Beacon

I

199

South Wold

Earthwork

Fizgig Hole Plantation

Yorkshire Wolds Way

192

Earthwork

Spr

Spr

Centenary Way

Resr (dis)

Springs

Tumuli

High Bellmanear

Pit (dis)

197

Fizgig Hill

Spr

Pit (dis)

Tumuli

Screed Plantation

162

Wold Barn

H

Pit (dis)

Pit (dis)

192

Settrington Wood

Keeper's Cottage

Nine Spring Dale

Duggleby High Barn

Dugg Wo

Nine Springs Dale Plantation

Pit (dis)

Rabbit Slack

Pit (dis)

Wood House

Pits (dis)

Cinquefoil Hill

Fisher's Whin

Duggleby Dale Plantation

171

G

Whitestone Beck

The Peak

Spr

Spr

Sprs

Pit (dis)

Broad Balk

73

Spr

The Sikes

Cowcliff Hill

157

86

High St

87

Duggleby Wold

ston Hill

172

165

Contours are given in metres
The vertical interval is 5m

1 km or ½ mile
B1253 Duggleby

105

Follow the clear path slanting down the hill and go straight on, reaching a metalled lane **J** that passes Rowgate Farm. After one mile (1.6 km) turn right at a small reservoir **K** and follow the bridleway along the edge of the first field, cross the middle of the second field before crossing Wintringham Beck to reach the village.

Turn left and follow the road past the last house and then double back right along a rough lane **L**. Follow this path towards St Peter's Church **39**, which, although usually locked, is still worth a detour. This is one of the most interesting churches on the National Trail and is rather big for a small village such as Wintringham It is constructed from the same seam of Tadcaster

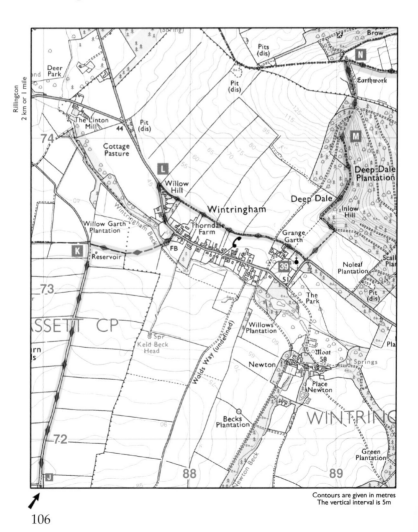

Contours are given in metres
The vertical interval is 5m

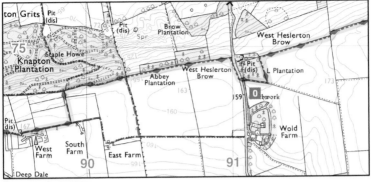

Contours are given in metres
The vertical interval is 5m

limestone that was used to build York Minster and its most fascinating feature is the stained-glass windows of the aisle, each one depicting a 14th-century saint on a white background stained yellow. Such rich glaziery is considered rare outside York. The carving of the pews, pulpit and screens is Jacobean. The well-preserved church is mainly 14th and 15th century.

Seek out, also, the following instruction to bellringers provided by Michael Gill, the clerk, in 1723:

> I pray you Gentlemen beware
> And when you ring ye Bells take care;
> For he that Rings and breaks a stay,
> Must pay Sixpence without delay.
> And if you ring in Spurs or Hatt
> You must likewise pay Sixpence for that.

Just before reaching the church the Yorkshire Wolds Way turns sharp left up the field side to enter Deep Dale Plantation, which is one of the oldest Forestry Commission operations in the Wolds. On entering the wood turn left on the forest track and where it swings sharply to the left, turn sharp right up a short but very steep climb **M**. Follow the old earthwork until you reach a farm track. Turn left and very soon right to enter the woods of Knapton Plantation **N**. From this point the north–south walking is virtually at an end; from now on, the primary direction will be west–east. This is West Heslerton Brow and at a suitable spot, in clear weather, you may catch your first glimpse of the North Sea. When you reach a lane **O**, make a minor detour round a small plantation masking an old pit and continue to head east with a fence on your left.

107

Just after passing Manor Wold Farm the path crosses a lane and continues ahead over the fields. After several short 'ups and downs' it again reaches a tarmac lane **P** down which the route turns left. In a short distance look out for a signpost on the right which offers a field edge path parallel to, but above the road. This makes for easier and safer walking. Rejoin the road a little further on and continue down into Sherburn **40**, passing on your right the continuation of the Yorkshire Wolds Way to Filey.

Wharram Percy

The original route of the Yorkshire Wolds Way bypassed what is by far one of the most interesting historical features to be seen along the footpath. Fortunately, the present route passes right through the middle of this fascinating site. Wharram Percy **35** is the best preserved ruin of a deserted medieval village in England. If walking from Thixendale to Sherburn in a day, allow at least an hour to explore and savour the peace. Close your eyes and allow your imagination to wander.

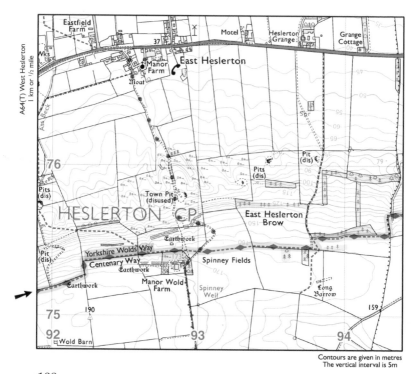

Contours are given in metres
The vertical interval is 5m

Wharram Percy (the name is derived from the old Scandinavian *hwerhamm*, which means 'at the bends', and from the Percys who were lords of the manor in the 12th–14th centuries) was built in the beautifully tranquil Deep Dale. There is evidence of at least one Iron Age house (*c.* 100 BC) having existed here, as well as a Roman farm or villa, but the village grew under Anglo-Saxon settlers. For three centuries it was a compact farming village, with 30 households, a population of 150, a church and a cemetery. However, by the mid-14th century, a combination of the Black Death and a change from corn-growing to sheep-rearing saw its population cut by half. The last house was deserted around the year 1500.

Today, the village is mainly a collection of bumpy earthworks. St Martin's Church contains much of its original 12th-century materials and is the most visible relic of Wharram Percy. Most of the village was on the hillside to the west and north of the church and it is possible to make out the grassed-over foundations of peasant houses, a manor house and mill. There is also a reconstructed pond. The site is maintained by English Heritage.

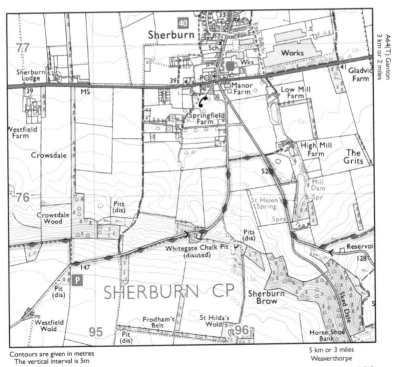

Contours are given in metres
The vertical interval is 5m

5 km or 3 miles
Weaverthorpe

One of the highlights of the Yorkshire Wolds Way, the deserted medieval village of Wha

cy is a haven of tranquillity in an already secluded landscape.

A CIRCULAR WALK FROM THIXENDALE

8¹/₂ miles (13.7 km)

Tranquil villages, unfrequented chalk valleys and one of the most picturesque Norman churches in the Wolds make this walk a consummate delight, especially on a fine day. Begin at Thixendale Post Office and walk up the road past Manor Farm. Bear left through a gate and follow the dry valley as it curves up to the left, then branch right up Milham Dale. Towards the top of the dale turn left along the farm track and on towards the metalled road. Follow this old Roman road and after two fields turn right down the hedge side to a stile. Continue downhill over a second stile and at the bottom of the hill turn left through a gate and continue ahead along the farm track to the metalled road.

Go up the hill for a short distance until you reach a signpost on the right. Cross the stile and follow an indistinct path

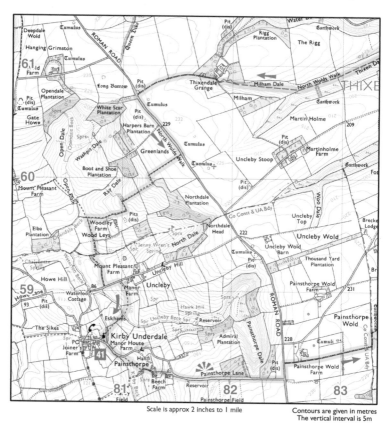

Scale is approx 2 inches to 1 mile

Contours are given in metres
The vertical interval is 5m

towards the church. Cross the bridge into the churchyard of All Saints' Church **41**, erected in the 12th century. Please respect this very special place and take time to explore a little of its history. A short detour to Kirby Underdale is also worth the effort of a few extra yards, especially if the tea shop is open!

Continue the walk down past the church for a short distance then turn right over a stile and across the field to a gate, turn left up the farm track which joins the metalled road. Go up the road, which offers splendid views to the rear, and at the T-junction turn left then right along the straight farm road. Where this turns sharp right, go straight ahead for about 30 yards (27 metres) then turn right down the hedge side and through a gate which leads down into Worm Dale. This path eventually joins the Yorkshire Wolds Way, which comes down the opposite grassy bank from Fridaythorpe. Turn left to join the National Trail and from here it is a pleasant, flat walk back to the village through Thixen Dale.

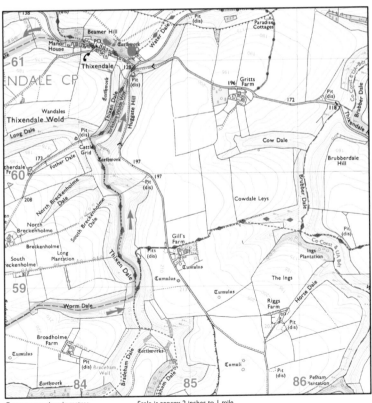

Contours are given in metres
The vertical interval is 5m

Scale is approx 2 inches to 1 mile

5 Sherburn to Filey

through Muston
14½ miles (22.9 km)

It may be tempting at first to put your head down on this final section and quickly reach the finishing post of the National Trail, followed perhaps by a hot bath and a celebratory drink. But then you will walk down Stocking Dale and, suddenly, feel pangs of regret that these fabulous chalk valleys are being left behind for good, and on the grand finale at Filey Cliffs there are few walkers who would not wish to savour the views of some of the finest coastal scenery in England. So by all means get your skates on through some of the more unexceptional field paths; it will allow time to appreciate the finer sections of the walk later on.

Sherburn is shot through by busy traffic heading to and from the coast, and the main place of interest is St Hilda's Church, which contains 11 Saxon stone sculptures.

Leave the village south from the main street, and rejoin the route either by going back up the right fork and taking the left turning through a field, or by cheating on a few steps of the Yorkshire Wolds Way and forking left to join the Way **A** on the tarmac lane leading to Butterwick, Foxholes and Weaverthorpe.

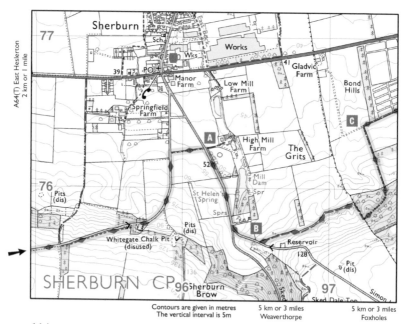

Contours are given in metres
The vertical interval is 5m

5 km or 3 miles
Weaverthorpe

5 km or 3 miles
Foxholes

Contours are given in metres
The vertical interval is 5m

High Mill, passed on the left, was a fine water-powered mill until well into this century.

Fork left up the lane **B** and in a short distance bear left along the field edge following the contour of the hill through scrub woodland. After a sharp right turn uphill, turn sharp left to follow a pleasant woodland path. Regrettably, after only a short distance this path swings downhill and back into the fields.

Turn sharp right **C** and follow the track past Manor Farm to a lane. After turning briefly right then left you continue along a limestone track to the next tarmac lane. Ganton Hall **43,** which is glimpsed through the trees farther up the hill, is Victorian and is often likened to a French château. Turn left down the lane towards Ganton **42,** with its whitewashed houses and a stream gurgling alongside the road and famous for its international golf course.

Turn right along Main Street and at the bend continue ahead with views of the magnificent 14th-century spire of St Nicholas Church on the left **44.** Continue ahead, the hedge now on your right. At the narrow plantation **D** turn sharp right up the hill.

Good signposts and waymarkers, stiles and wide field edges make for easy walking

ton Wold.

The path now takes several right and left turns before reaching the main road. A short distance to the left is a popular picnic spot with superb views and toilets.

Continue ahead past Grange Farm. This is a private road but also a public footpath which continues for about a mile (1.6 km) before turning right to pass RAF Staxton Wold **45**. Continue downhill past High Farm and where the track begins to level out look out for a path on the left which climbs steeply uphill **E**. With only one short right then left turn the path goes straight ahead along field borders crossing the heads of two small dry valleys before reaching a tarmac road **F**.

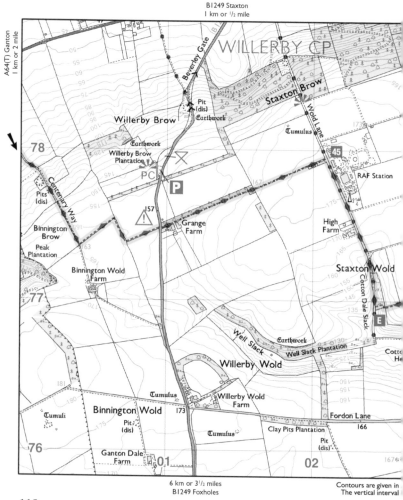

Turn right for about 350 yards (320 metres) then left to follow the field edge path above Raven Dale. Keep the hedge or fence hard on your right-hand side as the path curves around the head of Camp Dale **G** before finally dropping downhill to The Camp **46**.

Why, you might ask, does the path not simply follow the floor of these lovely valleys? The answer may be staring you in the face! Bulls run in these fields and footpaths specially created for the Yorkshire Wolds Way National Trail were drawn along the safer valley tops. Remember, bulls are bigger than you – and can run faster!

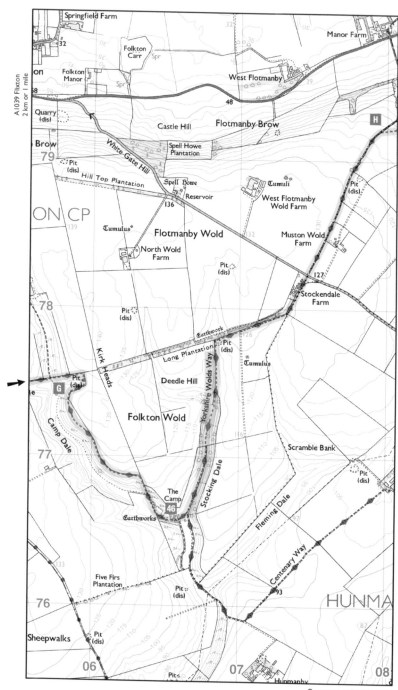

Springfield Farm

Manor Farm

Folkton Carr

Spr

West Flotmanby

Folkton Manor

Spr

A1039 Flixton
2 km or 1 mile

on

58

48

H

Quarry (dis)

Castle Hill

Flotmanby Brow

Brow

79

White Gate Hill

Spell Howe Plantation

Pit (dis)

Hill Top Plantation

Spell Howe

Tumuli

Reservoir

West Flotmanby Wold Farm

136

ON CP

139

Tumulus*

Flotmanby Wold

132

Muston Wold Farm

North Wold Farm

127

Pit (dis)

Stockendale Farm

78

Pit (dis)

Earthwork

126

Pit (dis)

Kirk Heads

Long Plantation

Tumulus*

G

Pit (dis)

Deedle Hill

Yorkshire Wolds Way

Camp Dale

Folkton Wold

Scramble Bank

77

Stocking Dale

Pit (dis)

The Camp

46

Earthworks

Fleming Dale

Five Firs Plantation

Pit (dis)

93

HUNMA

76

Centenary Way

87

Sheepwalks

Pit (dis)

06

Pit

07

Hunmanby

08

Contours are given in metres
The vertical interval is 5m

Contours are given in metres
The vertical interval is 5m

Hunmanby

The Camp **46** lies at the junction of Camp Dale and Stocking Dale and is the site of one of the many deserted medieval villages to be found in the Yorkshire Wolds. Little can be seen today apart from an old dew pond and some grassed over mounds.

The Yorkshire Wolds Way now turns left up Stocking Dale. An alternative and, after wet weather, a generally drier route into Filey follows the Centenary Way down the valley and is described in the circular walk from Filey (pages 126–7).

Follow the track up the dale and through Stockendale Farm. Cross the main road and continue ahead along the field edge track and after about ³/₄ of a mile (1.2 km) bear right **H** to follow a cross-field path to a stile in the hedge on the far side of the field.

The field path now descends the chalk scarp towards Muston **47** with good views right to the chalk cliffs of Speeton and Bempton. Turn right to follow the road through the village and just before the end of the village a short loop road on the left gives access to a path on the right of the terrace of houses **I**, crosses two fields and then the main A165 Scarborough–Bridlington road.

Walk down past the school playing field and turn right **J** to join the main road into Filey. There are several ways of passing through Filey to reach the end of the Yorkshire Wolds Way. The quickest way to reach the sea is to turn left then almost instantly turn right down Grange Avenue, swinging right along Clarence Drive. Pass under the railway and continue ahead to the seafront. Alternatively, turn left along the main road into the town and go straight ahead after passing the bus station to drop steeply downhill to the shore.

At the foot of Church Ravine **48** a flight of steps opposite the toilets leads up onto the cliff top, from where you can make your way through the Country Park **50** to the sculpture which marks the end of the Yorkshire Wolds Way and also the

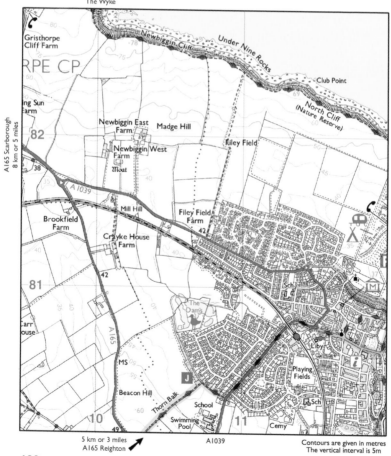

Cleveland Way. If the tide is low, an attractive alternative route passes the lifeboat station and follows the beach beneath Pampletine Cliffs **49** and along the rocks towards Filey Brigg **51**. A path ascends the cliff a short distance before the clay cliff terminates and once on the cliff top it is only a short distance back to the sculpture. From near here there are magnificent views northwards towards Scarborough and Robin Hood's Bay, and to the south, beyond the wide sweep of Filey Bay, rise the dramatic chalk cliffs of Bempton. At 400 feet high (122 metres) these cliffs are home to thousands of nesting razorbills, guillemots and puffins, as well as being the only mainland breeding site of the gannet in England.

If you have a day to spare, take the Bridlington bus as far as Speeton and then follow the path through the church car park and over fields to walk the cliff path along these superb chalk cliffs to a grand finish at Flamborough, surely a fitting climax to your walk along the backbone of the Yorkshire Wolds!

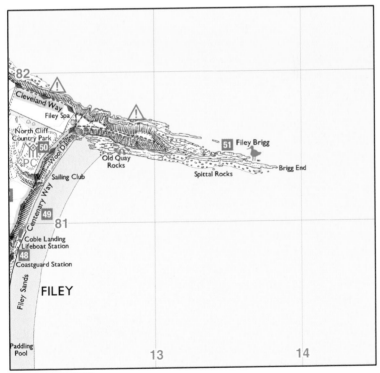

Contours are given in metres
The vertical interval is 5m

Filey

For many, Filey is the most attractive spot on the Yorkshire coast: a seaside town delightfully free of the worst excesses of holiday resorts, a magnificent bay well sheltered for bathing, windsurfing and yachting, with dramatic views of the chalk headland at Flamborough and Bempton in one direction and the great black finger of Filey Brigg in the other. Add the atmosphere of a traditional Yorkshire fishing village and its unique 'coble' boats, and you have an interesting place.

Filey grew as a fishing community well before the Norman Conquest, and the fishing craft seen at the Coble Landing, flat-bottomed for beach-launching, have their roots in the Viking longboats that were a common sight on this coast more than a thousand years ago. They are used for line fishing for white fish such as cod, haddock and plaice, and for the laying of 'fleets' of crab and lobster pots along the rocky shore.

The Georgian-style houses in the Crescent, overlooking the bay, were built in 1840 when Filey enjoyed brief prosperity as a spa town using mineral waters tapped on the cliffs above the Brigg. The most interesting part of town is in the Queen Street area. Look for the old house at the end of the street, close to the cliff edge, that was once called T'awd Ship Inn and was the haunt of smugglers.

Filey Brigg

There is no geological curiosity on the English coast quite like Filey Brigg **51**. At low tide the jagged reef, a $^3/_4$-mile (1.2-km) protrusion forming an almost perfect right-angle to the bay, has the appearance of an aborted attempt at building a causeway across the North Sea. Thousands of years ago, a huge layer of clay was deposited on this coast by the action of glaciers, but it quickly eroded to expose a solid floor of lower calcareous grit stone that Scandinavian settlers named *bryggja*, meaning landing place.

It may look like a natural jetty on a calm summer's day, but the Brigg is carefully avoided by all craft, big and small, at any time of year. The coastal currents are fierce, onshore winds can be strong and many vessels have been shipwrecked on its black teeth. Anglers have also been swept away by the ferocious breakers. When the seas are high and visibility is poor it must be considered out of bounds, and walkers should always take

Journey's End: the cliffs north of Filey Brigg, with Scarborough in the distance.

care on the cliff in mist, high winds and, most important of all, at high tide.

The Brigg is very popular with birdwatchers, who see many rarities making landfall during the autumn and spring migration periods. Winter visitors that are frequently seen off-shore include long-tailed ducks, red-throated divers and red-necked grebes. In the summer there are many gannets, kitti-wakes and auks to be seen fishing nearby, as well as common and arctic terns. The small building at the foot of the clay cliffs is used by local ornithologists as a hide for watching the numerous birds that settle on or pass by the Brigg. This is a twitcher's paradise!

The cliff above the Brigg, known as Carr Nase, was the site of a Roman signal station, one of a series that stretched from Flamborough in the south to Scarborough, Ravenscar and beyond to the north. They performed an 'early warning' func-tion, watching for a Viking invasion and preparing to relay the warning by a series of beacons to Eboracum, the great Roman city that is now York.

A CIRCULAR WALK FROM FILEY

10 miles (17 km)

This excellent walk starts at the Coble Landing in Filey and re-
traces the route of the Yorkshire Wolds Way through Muston
before climbing the chalk escarpment to Stockendale Farm.
Follow the Yorkshire Wolds Way down Stocking Dale and on
reaching The Camp, leave the Yorkshire Wolds Way and continue
down the valley following the route of the Centenary Way. After
walking for about 700 yards (640 metres) a limestone track strikes
up the valley side. Towards the top of the hill turn sharp left and

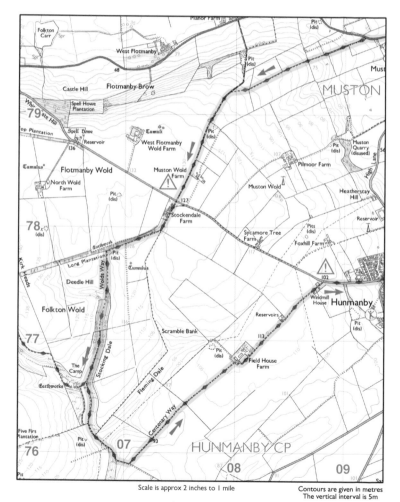

Scale is approx 2 inches to 1 mile

Contours are given in metres
The vertical interval is 5m

126

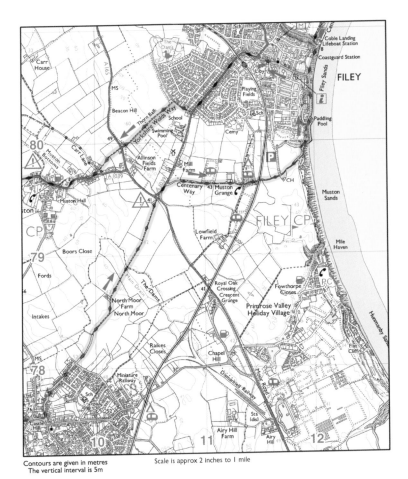

Contours are given in metres
The vertical interval is 5m

Scale is approx 2 inches to 1 mile

follow the path across the fields, pass to the right of Field House Farm and at the main road turn right towards Hunmanby. Just beyond the roundabout turn left along Northgate and, where it ends, continue ahead along the track.

Pass to the right of North Moor Farm and on reaching the main road, cross with care and follow the Filey road for a short distance before turning right along the road to Muston Grange Caravan Park. Go straight ahead, cross the railway line, pass the golf club and the path emerges on the cliff edge, with magnificent views around the whole of Filey Bay from the Brigg in the north to the high chalk cliffs of Speeton and Bempton to the south-east. The path drops down to the promenade which you can follow to return to the start of the walk.

The dramatic clay cliffs and long, rocky finger of Filey Brigg.

PART THREE

USEFUL INFORMATION

Transport

The southern section of the Yorkshire Wolds Way between Hull and Market Weighton is well served with a regular bus service operated mainly by East Yorkshire Motor Services. The northern section from Malton to Filey is also generally well served by Yorkshire Coastliner. Within the Wolds, however, public transport is somewhat sparse. Trains run between Hull and Filey and are most likely to be used at the beginning and end of the continuous walk.

Buses

In addition to the services mentioned above, the Wolds Way Project operates a Woldsbus service on a limited number of days during the holiday season. This closely follows the line of the Yorkshire Wolds Way and is useful for both walkers and those wishing to explore the more remote corners of the Yorkshire Wolds. The continuation of this service is subject to the availability of further funding. A regular seasonal service from Hull across the Wolds to Malton and on to Thornton Dale is also organised by the North York Moors National Park Authority.

Trains

Hull can be reached via Doncaster from the south, York from the north, and Leeds from the west. An east coast line operates between Hull, Filey and Scarborough. If you walk south to north (as described in this book) you can use the train to return from Filey to Hull. Regular trains also run between Scarborough, via Malton, to York, where you can join the mainline network.

Ferries

European visitors arriving in Hull by ferry from the continent should travel to Hull Station from where there are regular trains to Hessle and the start of the Yorkshire Wolds Way. From Hessle Station cross the bridge to the south and turn right on Redcliff Road, then left down Cliff Road to join the Yorkshire Wolds Way at the sculpture on the banks of the Humber.

Travel Information

Public transport timetables and information throughout Yorkshire can be obtained by ringing 0870 608 2 608, or log on to www.yorkshiretravel.net

Accommodation

At the Humber and coastal ends of the Yorkshire Wolds Way accommodation is plentiful but is less so deep in the Yorkshire Wolds. The five sections of the footpath described in this book make the best use of the bed and breakfast/meal facilities on offer, but there are a number of other off-route places at which it is possible to spend the night, and you may wish to lengthen or shorten your day's walking accordingly.

The Wolds Way Project issues an Accommodation and Information Guide which details the full range of accommodation available on or close to the route of the walk. It is highly advisable to book ahead as accommodation can become booked up, especially during May and the summer months. Please remember to give accommodation providers advance notice if you require an evening meal, packed lunch or wish to bring a pet with you.

The Accommodation and Information Guide may be obtained from the Wolds Way Project, c/o North York Moors National Park Authority, Bondgate, Helmsley, York YO62 5BP. Tel +44(0) 1439 770657. Details are also available on the Yorkshire Wolds Way website www.woldsway.gov.uk

Camping

In view of the fact that virtually every step of the Yorkshire Wolds Way is on agricultural land, official campsites are few and *ad hoc* pitches, of the sort one finds on wilder paths like the Pennine Way, are non-existent. Some farmers allow camping on their land by responsible people and it is worth while using the Ordnance Survey maps to pinpoint farms near to your planned overnight stops and writing to the farmer asking for permission or, if he does not allow camping, for advice on whether his neighbours do (do not forget the s.a.e.). The facilities may be basic but a water supply should be available. Never camp anywhere without seeking permission.

Tourist Information Centres

Tourist Information Centres, run by local authorities in the area of the Yorkshire Wolds and beyond, are the best sources of general information when planning your visit to the area. On the Yorkshire Wolds Way itself there are two TICs – near the beginning, at the Humber Bridge, and near the end, in Filey.

Interlocking spurs indicate that a fast-flowing stream once coursed down Horse Dale ne

Haythorpe.

Others cover wide areas of the countryside through which the footpath passes.

Beverley TIC, 34 Butcher Row, Beverley, East Yorkshire HU17 0AB. Tel: 01482 867430.

Bridlington TIC, 25 Prince Street, Bridlington, East Yorkshire YO15 2NP. Tel: 01262 673474.

Filey TIC, John Street, Filey, North Yorkshire YO14 9DW. Tel: 01723 518000.

Hull TIC, 1 Paragon Street, Hull HU1 3NA. Tel: 01482 223559.

Humber Bridge TIC, North Bank Viewing Area, Ferriby Road, Hessle HU13 0LN. Tel: 01482 640852.

Malton TIC, 58 Market Place, Malton, North Yorkshire. Tel: 01653 600048.

Scarborough TIC, Pavilion House, Valley Bridge Road, Scarborough, North Yorkshire. Tel: 01723 373333.

Local facilities

Many Wolds villages are classic examples of settlements where rural services have steadily declined. Useful facilities do exist but they are not numerous. Most pubs do meals or snacks at lunchtime and in the early evening. Some villages have just one bus service per week and these are not included in this list.

Further details of amenities can be obtained where there is a tourist information centre (TIC), through a personal visit, letter or telephone call (see addresses above). Further facilities are marked on the maps. Rural services are constantly under review and some may be withdrawn while others, from time to time, might be added. Some of the village post offices have limited opening times. Along the footpath, it is always worth asking a farmer or fellow-walker the whereabouts of a facility that you require.

Hull: all facilities
Hessle: all facilities (TIC at Humber Bridge viewing area)
North Ferriby: bus, café, PO, pub, shop, takeaway food, tel.
Welton: bus, PO, pub, shop, tel.
Brantingham: bus, PO, pub, shop, tel.
South Cave: bus, PO, pub, shop, takeaway food, tel.
North Newbald: bus, PO, pub, shop, takeaway food, tel.
Goodmanham: pub, tel.
Market Weighton: bus, PO, pub, shops, café, takeaway food, tel.

Nunburnholme: tel.
Londesborough: tel.
Pocklington: bus, PO, pub, shops, café, takeaway food, tel.
Millington: pub, café, restaurant, tel.
Huggate: pub, shop, café, tel.
Fridaythorpe: bus, café, pub, shop, restaurant, tel.
Thixendale: café, PO, pub, shop, takeaway food, tel.
Wharram le Street: tel.
Wintringham: tel.
Sherburn: bus, PO, pub, shop, tel.
Ganton: bus, pub, tel.
Muston: bus, pub, shop, tel.
Filey: all facilities

Useful addresses and telephone numbers

Countryside Agency, John Dower House, Crescent Place, Cheltenham, Glos GL50 3RA. Tel: 01242 521381. email: info@countryside.gov.uk

Countryside Agency, Yorkshire & Humberside Region, 4th Floor, Victoria Wharf, No 4 The Embankment, Sovereign Street, Leeds LS1 4BA. Tel: 0113 246 9222.

East Riding of Yorkshire Council, County Hall, Beverley HU17 9BA. Tel: 01482 887700. email: info@eastriding.gov.uk (Responsible for the East Riding section of the Yorkshire Wolds Way)

North Yorkshire County Council, Highways & Transportation Dept, Area Office, Southgate, Pickering, North Yorkshire YO18 8BL Tel: 01751 472031 (Responsible for the North Yorkshire section of the Yorkshire Wolds Way)

North Yorkshire & Cleveland Coastal Forum, c/o North York Moors National Park Authority, Bondgate, Helmsley, York YO62 5BP. Tel: 01439 770657. email: info@northyorkmoors-npa.gov.uk

Ordnance Survey, Romsey Road, Maybush, Southampton SO16 4GU. Tel: 08456 050505 email: customerservices@ordsvy.gov.uk

Ramblers' Association, 2nd Floor, Camelford House, 87–90 Albert Embankment, London SE1 7TW Tel: 020 7339 8500. email: ramblers@london.ramblers.org.uk (Publishes *The Rambler's Year Book & Accommodation Guide*)

Wolds Way Project, c/o North York Moors National Park Authority, Bondgate, Helmsley YO62 5BP. Tel: 01439 770657. email: info@northyorkmoors-npa.gov.uk

The landmark church and spire of St Nicholas, Ganton.

Nearby places of interest

Bempton Cliffs Chalk precipice 400 ft (134 metres) high, an RSPB reserve where thousands of guillemots, razorbills, puffins, kittiwakes, fulmars, gannets, shags and cormorants nest.

Beverley The Minster (*c.* 1420) is one of Europe's most beautiful churches. There is also the Museum of Army Transport.

Bridlington A traditional seaside resort with some sophisticated modern attractions, such as 'Leisure World', a vast indoor pool including a surf machine. Also, Bayle Gate Museum in the Old Town is full of antiques, and there is an interesting harbour museum.

Burton Agnes A splendid late-Elizabethan mansion between Bridlington and Driffield. Has one of Yorkshire's most celebrated ghosts. Also, there are paintings by Gainsborough, Pissarro and Renoir, plus attractive gardens.

Flamborough Head Flamborough (derived from the 'flame' of beacons) is the best-preserved chalk headland in Britain. The breathtaking sea cliffs, at their highest point, are double the height of York Minster and since 1979 a 12-mile (19-km) stretch from Sewerby Steps to Black Cliff Nab, Speeton, has been defined as a Heritage Coast.

Hull The Maritime Museum tells the story of the port's whaling and fishing history; there is also a well-preserved 'Old Town', where the home of the slavery abolitionist William Wilberforce is a museum.

North Yorkshire Moors Railway A scenic 18-mile (29-km) line built by George Stephenson from Pickering to Goathland. It is a good way to see the National Park and well worth a detour.

Scarborough Noisy but, in places, elegant seaside resort with an interesting Norman castle, the grave of Anne Brontë in St Mary's churchyard, and plenty of entertainment.

Sewerby Sewerby Hall, a couple of miles north of Bridlington, has a collection of memorabilia from Amy Johnson, the Hull-born aviation pioneer. There is also a model village nearby.

Skidby Windmill Said to be the best surviving tower mill in England, it is a prominent landmark to the south of Beverley.

Sledmere Home of the Sykes family, the biggest landowners in the Yorkshire Wolds and also the people responsible for converting it from a vast sheep walk to prime arable land. The original Tudor building was replaced by today's structure, a splendid Queen Anne house.

York Specialises in 'wet weather' attractions, such as the Railway Museum, Jorvik Centre, Castle Museum, Yorkshire Museum, and York Minster, its south transept and famous rose window now beautifully restored after the 1984 fire.

Bibliography

There is a price to pay for the Yorkshire Wolds' unspoilt beauty and low profile among coach tour operators: unlike the North York Moors or the Yorkshire Dales, which both seem to support publishing empires, there are comparatively few books available about the Wolds, and most of the best are out of print. The following (far from complete) list will provide some suggestions for further reading for those whose appetite is whetted by a week rambling in the Wolds or just an evening spent leafing through this book.

Walking Guides

Six Circular Walks in the Yorkshire Wolds, East Riding of Yorkshire Council. Describes six walks of between 6 and 10 miles with map and points of interest.

Emett, Charlie, *Walking in the Wolds,* Cicerone. Describes 38 circular walks in East Yorkshire.

Graham, Uney, *Guide to Walking the Wolds.* A guide to discovering East Yorkshire on foot.

Vale of York & Yorkshire Wolds, Jarrolds – Pathfinder Guide.

Wallis, Ray, *The Minster Guide*, East Riding & Derwent R.A., 1999. A 50-mile (80-km) walk linking the Minsters of Beverley and York.

Wallis, Ray, *The Chalkland Way*, Hull R.A. A 40-mile (64-km) circular walk from Pocklington.

Walford, David F. *Yorkshire Wolds Wanderings*, Santona, 1997.

Chapman, Stephen, *Hudson's Way*, York Rail Press, 1986. The story of the York–Beverley railway.

Markham, L., *Pub Walks in East Yorkshire*, Countryside Books.

The East Yorkshire Village Book, Countryside Books. Describes over 130 villages in East Yorkshire

The gate to Sledmere Church, situated a few miles east of the Yorkshire Wolds Way.

General guide books

Allison, K. J., *The East Riding of Yorkshire Landscape*, Hodder & Stoughton, 1976. The definitive guide to the evolution of the Wolds landscape and the history of people in the Wolds.

Arnold, Sylvia M., *Wild Flowers of the Yorkshire Wolds*, Hutton Press, 1985. An interesting handbook to the flora of chalk landscape, with particular reference to many sites in the countryside through which the Yorkshire Wolds Way passes.

Elliot, Stephen C., *Bird Watching in East Yorkshire, The Humber and Teesmouth*, Hutton Press, 1989. Guide to species and bird watching sites in the Humber, Wolds and along the coast.

Gower, Ted, *Filey*, Dalesman Books, 1977. A short guide to the town that lies at the end of the Yorkshire Wolds Way, its fishing community and places of interest.

Pevsner, Nikolaus, *Buildings of England. Yorkshire: York and the East Riding*, Penguin, 1972. The standard reference work to architecture of the area, it is especially illuminating on parish churches throughout the Wolds. Essential reading for all interested in the built environment.

Waites, Bryan, *Exploring the Yorkshire Wolds*, Dalesman Books, 1984. Pocket gazetteer to the towns, villages and interesting features of East Yorkshire.

Wright, Geoffrey N., *The East Riding*, Batsford, 1976. An affectionate portrait of the area.

Fiction

Holtby, Winifred, *Anderby Wold*, Virago Press, 1981. The East Riding's own novelist started her regrettably short writing career with this excellent portrait of life in the Yorkshire Wolds, set around Rudston, near Bridlington.

Ordnance Survey Maps covering the Yorkshire Wolds Way

Four maps in the 'Explorer' (1:25 000) series cover the whole of the Yorkshire Wolds Way:

293	Kingston upon Hull & Beverley
294	Market Weighton & Yorkshire Wolds Central
300	Howardian Hills & Malton
301	Scarborough, Bridlington & Flamborough Head

The Ordnance Survey Road Map No 4 'Northern England' on a scale of 1 inch to 4 miles (1cm to 2.5km) is useful for reaching the Wolds from further afield.

Yorkshire Wolds Way Official Completion Book

Walkers who like to record the completion of their walk can sign the Completion Book at either the Country Park Stores at Filey Country Park, close to the finish of the route, or at the Tourist Information Centre on John Street, Filey.

Comments Please!

The Wolds Way Project Team are always happy to receive comments about the walk, whether good, bad or indifferent! Contact the National Trails Officer, c/o North York Moors National Park Authority, The Old Vicarage, Bondgate, Helmsley, York YO62 5BP. Tel: 01439 770657.

email: info@northyorkmoors-npa.gov.uk